What to Save from the '80s

WHAT TO SAVE FROM THE '80s

Charles J. Jordan

FAWCETT COLUMBINE • NEW YORK

To Donna, who scored 197,000 on Pac-Man.

A Fawcett Columbine Book
Published by Ballantine Books
Copyright © 1986 by Charles J. Jordan

All rights reserved under International and Pan-American
Copyright Conventions. Published in the United States by
Ballantine Books, a division of Random House, Inc., New York,
and simultaneously in Canada by Random House of Canada
Limited, Toronto.

Permissions acknowledgments may be found at the end of this book.

Library of Congress Catalog Card Number: 86-90736

ISBN: 0-449-90186-6

Cover photo by David Spindell
Text design by Michaelis/Carpelis Design Associates

Manufactured in the United States of America
First Edition: October 1986
10 9 8 7 6 5 4 3 2

CONTENTS

What to Save from the '80s

Introduction

Let's say that suddenly you find yourself endowed with the ability to return to the 1950s, '40s, or '30s. You are given a box to take with you to fill with items from your backward journey in time. What sort of things will you decide to put in this box?

If you go back to 1955, you may pick up a few early Elvis Presley Sun records. Perhaps you'll go to Chicago to get a copy of the *Chicago Tribune* on the day in 1948 when it erroneously announced "Dewey Defeats Truman." If 1938 is your destination, you can't do better than to buy Action Comics Number 1—featuring the debut of Superman. All you'll spend on your journey is pocket change, yet you'll return with a cache of goods worth thousands of dollars today.

Now let's imagine instead that your objective is to fill the same box with objects from the 1980s—brand-new items that can be magically transported to the far future for presentation to your great-grandchildren on their fortieth birthdays. What kinds of memorabilia will you choose to save for them, in the hope of seeing a huge appreciation in value?

Predicting the future has always been a risky affair, especially when it is done in the collectibles field. The plain truth is that there are a great many variables that might sway the value of an object by thousands of dollars—variables that are yet to materialize. Who in the early 1950s could have imagined that a singing truck driver from Memphis would go on to change the course of popular music? And what foolhardy soothsayer of the late '30s would have publicly predicted that a character called "Superman" would capture the fancy of three generations?

Collecting for tomorrow is 25 percent crystal ball, 75 percent collecting know-how. Once you come to understand the latter, the odds are in your favor. Figuring out the future values of memorabilia involves a lot of hindsight. Certain trends repeat themselves over and over again. In this decade, for example, there has already been an incident quite similar to the famous "Dewey Defeats Truman" headline (current value: over

$1000). You can get today's version, however, for about $50. (More on that later.) The point is, opportunity is knocking at every corner. All you have to do is figure out when to open the door.

As we head into the last years of the 1980s, we can already look back at the early years of this hectic decade and see a cavalcade of tomorrow's collectibles lining up before our very eyes—recent memorabilia taking every form from a Royal Wedding coin and *Raiders of the Lost Ark* souvenir movie magazine to many items you never even realized existed. Which among these items are worth saving? What will our children and grand-children be seeking from our decade further on down the collecting road?

The purpose of this book is to sneak a look into the future, view the by-products of modern-day America, and learn to know which ones to collect. We have posed the question "What are you saving from the 1980s?" to some of the country's leading specialty experts, as well as to amateur collectors across the United States who are at this very moment stockpiling memorabilia in quiet anonymity. The results are presented with the hope that, starting today, you too will begin looking differently at the items all around us.

1. The Printed Word

Newspapers

In times of national and international events of sudden magnitude, people turn to those tangible chroniclers, the newspapers. The idea of saving newspapers goes back a long way. So popular were newspapers reporting the assassination of President Abraham Lincoln that for decades there was a lucrative enterprise awaiting anyone with a printing press who could run off reproductions.

History's Big Moments

In this century, the beginning and end of World War II and the death of Franklin Roosevelt have been popular headlines for collectors. The stockpiling of newspapers did not become a major force, however, until two events of the 1960s created a rush to the newsstands. It would be difficult to find a person who hadn't saved (and still is saving) headlines announcing the death of President John F. Kennedy or the first landing of men on the Moon. I count myself among this group. I remember watching the CBS coverage of the landing of Apollo 11 in July 1969, when sometime in the middle of the night Walter Cronkite held up the famous front page of the *New York Times,* hot off the press, with the simple but startling headline: "Men Walk On Moon." Cronkite even mentioned that here was an item to put aside for our great-grandchildren. For countless Americans, those few moments of national airtime precipitated hours of frantic searching the next morning. As I was in Southport, Connecticut, at the time, I figured I had a good chance of picking up a *New York Times* with the certain-to-be-collectable headline. My mistake was not getting up early enough. I remember starting my search through newspaper stores along the Post Road around 6:30 A.M. At every store I stopped at, the *Times* had been sold out "hours ago." I had to be content bringing home copies of *Waterbury Republican* and *Hartford Courant.*

Final Editions

While first and last editions of magazines often command impressive paybacks to collectors only a few decades after their issue, not so the case with newspapers. This is the opinion of Rick Brown, editor of a journal called *Newspaper Collectors* (Box 19134, Lansing, MI 48901). He advises people not to waste their time with commemoratives or final editions of newspapers. "The passage of time does not increase their value significantly," he said. The final edition of the *New York Herald-Tribune,* issued in the '60s, a much ballyhooed event at the time, will barely fetch a few dollars among serious newspaper collectors today. This feeling was echoed by noted historic newspaper authority Mark E. Mitchell of Alexandria, Virginia. "Thus far, the only newspapers I have personally put away for the future from the '80s are several D.C. papers reporting on the 1980 Reagan victory, four copies of the final *Washington Star,* and the first issue of the *Washington Times.* Of these issues, I feel that the Reagan election will be the most valuable in the future."

Regardless, when newspapers do fold, people scramble around frantically buying up copies and creating, justifiably or not, a fast market for them; sometimes it lasts only a few hours, or it might continue for months until reality settles in.

This happened with both the *Philadelphia Bulletin* and the *Washington Star* when they ceased publication early in the decade.

In the case of the *Washington Star,* a few quick-witted people made some big money in a short period of time. It all began on Friday, August 7, 1981, when the newspaper ended 128 years of service. After reporting losses of $20 million a year, Time, Inc., which purchased the foundering newspaper in 1978, finally decided to pull the plug that summer. When the last issue of the *Star* hit the newsstands that day, it carried a cover cost of 20 cents a copy. By the following Monday, copies were being resold by the public for as much as $200 each. "My husband bought fifty copies of the paper that first day for twenty cents each," Leila Head of Washington, D.C., told me. "He literally ran after the delivery truck as it was making its morning rounds." Mrs. Head said that they sold about half the copies that same day for $20 apiece. "We decided to hold on to the rest for a few days and see what they'd go for," she added. "Then we placed a few ads and managed to sell another fifteen for $200 each by the week's end."

News of the profiteering infuriated the outgoing brass at the *Star*, and the newspaper went back on press with its final edition in an effort to create a glut of newspapers and bring down the demand, popping the bubble created by the paper's demise. Ultimately, it worked. "Newspapers, like everything else, are worth whatever a person is willing to pay for them at the moment," remarked Charles Smith, secretary of the International Newspaper Collector's Club. "In the case of the final edition of the *Washington Star* or the *Philadelphia Bulletin*, the highest prices were realized immediately after the papers folded," he explained. "After the dust settles, people realize the enormous number of copies distributed and the prices begin to go down." This explains why the final edition of the *Star*, of which over 330,000 copies were printed, showed up within six months after the paper's discontinuation for as little as $5 and $10 at flea markets. "Almost everyone saved their copies," Smith explained.

Best Sections to Save

Well then, what should you save? "For one, I'd save any Sunday color comics section," said Brown of *Newspaper Col-lectors*. "There are scores of thousands of Sunday color comics section collectors out there and the ranks are growing daily. Thus, Sunday color comics sections from as recently as the late '60s are bringing $1 to $2 each, while prices for World War II comics bring a minimum of $5 each, with some going as high as $10 to $15 each." Looking ahead, Brown predicted that if a person were to save one of each week's Sunday color comic sections for the next thirty-five years, they could expect to part with the heap of paper someday for at least $1500 (using today's appreciation scale as a basis). "Not bad for something you pay for anyway and then just throw away." Another candidate for the closet would be the sports pages of the same paper, he said, "provided there is good national coverage and not local only."

Historic Headlines

For those who don't have the space to save all this paper, Brown advises that people concentrate on potentially historic headlines as they happen. "In general, the more major the event and the more international the implications are, the more collector value it commands," he explained. He advised collectors to select events destined to make the history books and cites examples of past headlines now commanding premium values: the disappearance of Amelia Earhart, Lindbergh's flight, the bombing of Pearl Harbor. As a rule of thumb, he said that if you have a choice of newspapers confronting you on the newsstand, go for the one with the largest headline type, across the top. "If the headline is small, it will hurt the collector value."

Brown's prognostications for the '80s include the assassination of Anwar Sadat, the Iranian hostage crisis, "any and all space-related papers" (including coverage of the Shuttle missions and the Shuttle *Challenger* tragedy), and the 1985 earthquake in Mexico City, to cite a few. Mark Mitchell adds that he has already seen Cincinnati newspapers reporting on Pete Rose breaking Ty Cobb's hit record on sale for $25 each. Brown suggests that one make use of the evening network newscasts in gauging the impact of an event while in progress. "The longer time span the event makes the national news, the more collector value it will have." He said that if one were to start saving newspapers from these three categories—comics, sports, and historic headlines—"you'd have an attic filled after forty years, but you could sell the entire hoard for somewhere in the neighborhood of $5000 to $10,000."

Watch for "Bloopers"

The most desirable papers of the '80s may turn out to be neither final editions nor historic front pages, but instead "error headlines," or printed newspaper bloopers of the worst order. The greatest error headline of all time is the famous "Dewey Defeats Truman" classic goof from the 1948 Presidential campaign. The incorrect headline of the *Chicago Tribune* gained international recognition via Frank Cancellare's widely circulated wire service picture of a grinning and triumphant Truman on the rear platform of the Presidential train, holding the paper aloft after his stunning upset victory over Republican challenger Thomas Dewey.

No press photographers happened to capture the '80s version of over-eager journalism at work during the heat of a political campaign, yet the opportunity was there again in 1980—in fact twice. As devoted convention-watchers may recall, at one point during the Republican National Convention that year it appeared briefly that former President Gerald Ford was about to accept the Vice-Presidential spot with party nominee Ronald Reagan. This speculation came late in the evening, just as the nation's newspapers were readying their morning editions for press. While most newspapers held up their front pages until things looked a bit more certain, at least two dailies decided to take a chance and scoop the nation. Before the night was through, Ford had turned down the offer and George Bush was chosen for the VP spot.

"It's Reagan and Ford" announced the *Chicago Sun-Times* and the *Call Chronicle* of Allentown, Pennsylvania, the following morning. Today, copies of those two papers can sell for as much as $50 apiece. "It's viewed in the same way as the famous 'Dewey Defeats Truman' headline," said newspaper collector Mitchell. "Collectors like errors, and the Dewey/Truman headline is today considered the most popular twentieth-century paper to be had." Mitchell said it now sells for over $1000 a copy. One can expect the stock of the Reagan/Ford papers to appreciate as Reagan gets a more firm footing in the history books. An interesting

example of the caution of the venerable *New York Times* during the heat of elections can be seen on their front page the morning after Ronald Reagan's crashing victory over Democrat Walter Mondale (in case you've forgotten, it was Reagan in fifty states, Mondale zip). The *Times* showed its traditional restraint by announcing, "Reagan The Apparent Victor."

In the event that all this has you scurrying down to the local newsstand in anticipation of some pin money for your retirement, Brown advises the following regarding storage:

Store papers flat and in the open position. ("Do not leave them folded in half! Papers that are stored for many years in the folded position will get a brown stain at the half fold.")

Store papers in a box with a lid; ideal boxes for this purpose can be bought from litho-printers listed in the Yellow Pages. Brown said that boxes not only provide protection of the papers from sunlight and such, but also help overcome the "fire hazard" of having newspapers loosely stored in a confined area.

Magazines

Bloopers Here, Too

Magazines usually have more time to prepare their key stories, with deadlines that are more flexible than their newsprint counterparts. Occasionally, however, even a glossy trips up as it comes down to the wire on a fast-breaking news story. Twice I had an opportunity to see a magazine's cover with the earmarks of being one of the decade's best printed political mementoes. Even though it never reached the public, a few choice examples do exist, and every political and magazine collector worth his salt would give his eye teeth to add a copy to his collection. This gem is a cover of *Newsweek* magazine that shows Jimmy Carter victorious over Ronald Reagan during the 1980 Presidential election. The first copy I saw, in 1982, was framed and hanging on a wall at the plant of the Shenandoah Valley Press in Virginia. The photo showed President Carter rolling up his sleeves. The cover line implied that he was "Starting Over." I asked a plant employee about the cover and he said that the results were coming in just at the time *Newsweek* (which is printed at the Virginia plant)

was nearing presstime. To get around the tight deadline, *Newsweek* staffers prepared two covers, as well as two rough stories—one reporting a Reagan victory and the other telling of a Carter re-election. I meekly asked if by any chance there were any additional copies of this "conversation piece" lying about the plant that they might consider allowing me to add to my collection. Alas, no dice.

I forgot about the collectable cover until I found myself in the New York offices of *Newsweek* one day in 1985. There it was again—that cover, displayed on a wall. That's the closest I ever came to begging.

There are copies of *Time*

Time *magazine error cover.*

magazine in the hands of a few lucky collectors that its publishers would wish they didn't have. It's another example that mistakes can happen in the highest places. Late Sunday night, March 13, 1983, just as the March 21 edition of *Time* was being readied for distribution across the United States for Monday sales, staffers at the news magazine discovered that a teaser headline in the upper right-hand corner of the cover contained a mistake: an ''r'' in the word ''Control'' was missing from the line ''A New Plan For Arms Control.''

Andrew Check of Milwaukee, Wisconsin, was scanning the pages of the new national newspaper, *USA Today,* when he noticed an article detailing the *Time* error. ''Well, the wheels started turning,'' said Check. ''Knowing that 90 percent of the newsstands in Milwaukee receive their magazine shipments on Mondays, I figured that if *Time* didn't catch the mistake until Sunday night, there might be a chance that some copies might be on trucks.'' Check raced to his phone and called friends and relatives in a three-state area looking for a *Time* that carried the typo. *Time,* meanwhile, had tried hard to plug up its distribution channels to keep the error copies off the stands. When the mistake was discovered, printing schedules were scrambled, causing the publication to miss distribution deadlines. Consequently, many cities did not get their Monday *Time* allotments until Wednesday. Undaunted by *Time's* eleventh-hour footwork, Check called ''every newsstand in Milwaukee.'' On his second-to-the-last call he found his prize. ''Bingo! Now eleven issues reside in my safe deposit box,'' Check said.

Initial news reports indicated that no error copies were distributed, but, obviously, some did get through. Also, promotional ads that ran in many city newspapers, including *The New York Times,* carried a picture of the error cover, along with a slogan trumpeting *Time's* ability to get its advertisers' messages ''throughout the U.S. on Monday''—a most unfortunate bit of timing. As errors of this sort are forever popular, the future of this cover is guaranteed to hold a place as long as *Time* exists. Collectors might be able to name their own price should they find themselves the fortunate possessor of the original cover.

At the time of the catastrophic explosion of the

Space Shuttle *Challenger*, which took the lives of seven American astronauts, *The New Yorker* magazine was on press with its February 3, 1986 issue. News of the disaster prompted the publication to halt the presses as its editors were sent into a flurry of activity to modify a cartoon appearing on page 44. The cartoon featured a man seated at a barstool telling a companion, "I wish they'd shoot *my* congressman into space!" For all but the earliest copies of the magazine's more than half a million press run, the caption was rewritten to say, "I used to be a warm human being, but now, I'm sorry to say, I'm a bit of a swine."

"Special" Comic Books

One man who has been dealing with old magazines a long time is Walter Wakefield, the proprietor of the Antiquarian Old Book Store of Portsmouth, New Hampshire, who is widely known in the bibliophile field. In view of the fact that the first issues of such history-making journals as *National Geographic* and *Playboy* can command incredible sums (the first *NG* dated October 1888 fetches $5000 and the famous initial *Playboy* tops the $1500 mark), I asked Wakefield what he thought

might be the memorable magazines of the '80s. He surprised me by giving high grades to comic books published by Marvel with superhero themes. "Even though they cost on average 75 cents each new at present, the values seem to rise rapidly," he said. "I estimate 75 cent comics purchased now in this specific subject area will be worth three to ten times as much in ten years. Avid investors can get hold of distributors and buy quantities at healthy discounts—up to 40 percent off the cover in some cases."

Marvel issued what must stand as one of the most unusual issues in its long history during the decade when it came forth with a Pope John Paul II comic book in 1982. The idea had its genesis during the papal visit to Japan in February 1981. It was at that time that the Supreme Pontiff was presented with a Marvel comic featuring the life of St. Francis of Assisi. A few days later, Marvel's overseas representative received a surprise phone call from the Pope's official biographer, Father Mieczylslaw Malinski. "Could you write a comic book about the life of the Pope?" he asked, in all seriousness.

By the summer of 1982, Marvel had produced "The Life of

John Paul II," written by Steven Grant, drawn by John Tartaglione, and inked by Joe Sinnott. The full-color, sixty-four-page book tells the story of the Pope through the eyes of a fictional reporter who introduces himself on the first page by saying, "I'm a newspaper man—and the Pope is my beat!" His first job is to cover the Pope's appearance at Yankee Stadium in 1979. Impressed by the outpouring of affection shown this popular pope, the reporter begins looking into Pope John Paul II's life, tracing his infancy in Poland through the Nazi occu-

Move over Superman, here comes the Pope.

pation and Communist incursion, as well as the 1981 assassination attempt on his life. A Marvel spokesman said shortly before the comic's release that preliminary material was presented to the Pope for his review and, "The Pope loved it!"

How does one follow up a comic book on the Pope? In 1985, Marvel answered that question when it published a "Mother Teresa of Calcutta" comic book. Again, the "plot" featured a hardbitten reporter who was assigned to get the story, this time pursuing the seventy-five-year-old recipient of the Nobel Peace Prize. As he discovers, Mother Teresa is forever thinking of others. At one point she remarks in a word balloon, "That poor woman, being eaten by rats! I must help her!" The journalist sums it up with two words: "She cares." Shrewd collectors saw a future winner and stashed away scores of copies, selling for $1.25 on comic racks. The kids, however, seemed to prefer Spider Woman, and in the end Mother Teresa was not what you'd call a bestseller.

Cheesecake

On the other hand, Vanessa Williams was a bestseller. The verdict is still out on what the publication of pictures of the reigning Miss America in the buff (taken in her earlier years) did for Vanessa's career, but it is clear what it did for sales of the September 1984 issue of *Penthouse* magazine—they went through the ceiling. Bibliophile Walter Wakefield, however, does not hold out much of a future for Vanessa, who ultimately was forced to forfeit her crown as a result of the ordeal. "A lot of people bought up quantities of [that issue of] *Penthouse* at $4 per for investment," he said. He asked how many people could remember who she was even a year after the fact. (People who move from newsmaker status to prime candidates for a Trivial Pursuit question within a year's time have highly questionable collectable value.) Wakefield also pointed out that "a huge quantity" of the first Williams cover of *Penthouse* was printed—"much more than the regular printing," and equated the hoarding of these copies to the saving of equally mass-produced Susan B. Anthony dollars. "Anything issued in large quantity is not likely to be valuable in our lifetime," Wakefield opted.

New and Unusual Graphics
 Occasionally a mass-pro-duced magazine breaks the bank simply by being extraordinary. Such was the case when *National Geographic* magazine (circulation over 10 million) issued its first holographic cover, on its March 1984 issue. *National Geographic* was not the first magazine to experiment with a three-dimensional cover. Back in the '60s, *Venture* magazine issued 3-D images on its covers routinely via an expensive process called Xogroph, which involved gluing laminated plastic grid-sheets to its front covers. The *National Geographic* cover, run in conjunction with a story on holography, was the first to employ what is called a "laser-sculpted image," in this case depicting an eagle. Don Smith, a Louisville-based supplier of back copies of *National Geographic* to collectors and libraries for the past two decades, said that it is doubtful that the March '84 issue will soon become a hard-to-find item. He noted, however, that the increased number of library orders he's received, requesting additional copies of the hologram eagle issue, indicates that copies are repeatedly disappearing off library shelves. "This might lead one to believe that copies are already being considered

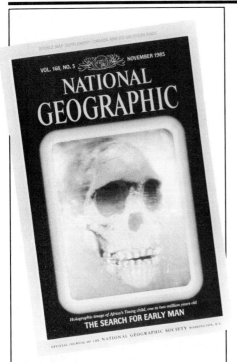

valuable to some people,'' Smith observed. ''This might also be an early clue that, with its unusual cover, it should be placed in a higher rate-structure [than other '80s *National Geographic* issues] as time goes by.'' In November 1985, the magazine issued its second holographic cover, this one even more stunning than the first. It featured a suspended skull dating back some one million years.

Books

The book field is always a prime proving ground for tomorrow's collectibles. First editions and other books of note have been collected by bibliophiles for centuries. It doesn't take long for the works of authors to appreciate in value. First-edition copies of Norman Mailer's *The Naked and the Dead,* with dust jacket, can already fetch between $250 and $325, while an original edition of Joseph Heller's *Catch-22,* in like condition, brings prices between $300 and $400. More rewards might be found, however, in searching for earlier books by today's bestselling authors, written when they were still struggling for recognition.

The recall of books by a publisher, usually because of factual errors, libelous material, or a charge of plagiarism, is by no means a common occurrence, but it does happen occasionally. Perhaps the most famous was the pulling in of the initial 2000 copies of Lewis Carroll's *Alice In Wonderland.* Of these, all but 48 were successfully taken out of circulation after the illustrator expressed displeasure with the reproduction quality of his work. The few that remained out of reach of the publisher have commanded remarkable sums in more than a century since they were produced.

Today, books about famous people, particularly female actresses, are vulnerable to recall. Celebrity books tend to increase in value quite quickly. The best ones are the scandal-type "unauthorized" editions. For a steady supply of these, watch remainder tables. While you're scouting, also look for remaindered quality art books, especially high-priced ones (over $40) about individual artists. Due to the high price not many were printed and copies will soon be in demand.

Parodies: Books, Magazines, Newspapers

A fun fad that swept through the print world during the first few years of the decade, only to halt as abruptly as it began, was the sudden profusion of periodical parodies. While the fun lasted, one could assemble a nifty collection of these journalistic jewels, most of which were well produced and rib-tickling in content. Because these parodies were designed to look strikingly similar to their intended targets, they often escaped the attention of the casual magazine browsers at newsstands, where most were marketed.

Printed parody has enjoyed a long history, and good contemporary parody can always be counted on to find a place in future collections. After all, these mimicking jesters document how a generation sees itself; what better way can a generation come to know its forebears than by seeing how they poked fun at themselves? Much of the credit for keeping the parody torch lit during the postwar years belongs to William Gaine's *Mad* magazine, debuting in August 1952 as a pure parody periodical. The first issue of *Mad* now sells for over $240. An early target of Gaines's brand of what he called "humor in the jugular vein" was the comics, which were enjoying runaway popularity during that decade. *Mad's* satires included "Believe It or Don't" ("Melvin Furd of Banff, Vt., is a Martian!" reads the caption below the drawing of a man) and "Poopeye" (about a muscle-bound sailor whose eye is forever popping out and ricocheting around the margins of the cartoon panels).

Parody in the early '80s relied for the most part on the efforts of a few adventurous entrepreneurs armed with printing presses who hit the market with lookalike periodicals that appear destined to enjoy a healthy future in collecting circles. One of the first was *Not The New York Times*, followed closely by *Off The*

Wall Street Journal, and *The Newark Times Book Review.* The latter, credited to an outfit calling itself Parody Publishing, Inc., and distributed by Tribeca Communications of New York, retailed for $5.95

when it appeared in 1982. Its listing of the bestsellers of the week poked fun at America's obsession with dieting and fitness books with titles such as *The I Love Hoboken Diet, Growing Up Obese,* and *Jane Fondue's Workbook.*

Magazines did not escape the barbs of parody during the period either. The staff of the *Harvard Lampoon* put out one of the best when they issued a takeoff of *People* magazine. To their credit, they got Brooke Shields to pose for the cover photo—holding a brook trout. Even some of the major publishing houses got into the act, with Crown Publishing of

Irrational Inquirer.

The Newark Times Book Review *parody.*

Not Quite TV Guide *spoofed the tube.*

New York releasing *Not Quite TV Guide* in 1983. That same year something called the *Irrational Inquirer* appeared, parodying—as you guessed—the *National Enquirer.* Sample stories included "You Can Call the Dead—Collect," "Woman Trapped in a Mason Jar For 10 Days" and "Victoria Principal Was a Blubber-Eating Eskimo." When it became difficult to tell the difference between the parody and the real thing, it was clear that the fad had pretty well played itself out.

2. Newsmakers

The Royal Wedding

The note stated simply that "The Lord Chamberlain is Commanded by The Queen and The Duke of Edinburgh" to request your presence at "the Marriage of His Royal Highness The Prince of Wales with The Lady Diana Spencer in St. Paul's Cathedral on Wednesday, 29th July, 1981 at 11:00 A.M." Dress, it pointed out, would be "Uniform, Morning Dress or Lounge Suit."

If you found the above invitation in your morning mail early in 1981, you were well on your way to collecting first-hand souvenirs stemming from what *Time* magazine called "the century's grandest royal match." Today these are the most prized of "tomorrow's heirlooms." If, on the other hand, you were among the majority of mortals on this side of the Atlantic who weren't invited, you had to be content to view the event on TV. During the day of the wedding, the three major networks pulled all stops, hitting the airwaves by 5:00 A.M. Eastern Time live from London (NBC jumped the competition by signing on at 4:30 A.M.) in time to provide coverage of the nuptials at 6:00 A.M. ET.

The last major Royal Wedding in this century was the marriage of Princess Elizabeth and Prince Philip back in 1947. Television was in its infancy at the time and could only replay newsreel footage a week after the fact. Television was ready for Prince Charles and Lady Di in 1981, however, sending its top news anchorpeople across the Atlantic to cover the glittering events that stretched out over the two miles between Buckingham Palace and St. Paul's Cathedral. ABC's coverage of the wedding was anchored by Peter Jennings and Barbara Walters, NBC's Tom Brokaw and Jane Pauley shared their coverage with "color" offered up by Peter Ustinov, while CBS and Dan Rather provided on-screen translations of the proceedings for the folks back home by David Frost and Lady Antonia Fraser.

From an international standpoint, no other single event of the '80s has eclipsed the televised pageantry of the wedding of Prince Charles and Princess Diana, nor the scope of souvenirs that flooded the market before, during, and

after. "The demand for Royal Wedding souvenirs was so great during the summer of 1981 that one woman told me she could have sold the dirt the couple walked over in St. James Park," said Dr. Wayne Swift, a psychologist and owner of the Royalty Bookshop in New York. During the height of Royal Wedding mania, when the "Lady Di Do" hairstyle became a rage among young women on both continents, items commercially marketed in this country and in Europe ranged from reproductions of Lady Di's engage-

Lady Di doll: one of many Royal Wedding items available.

Replica of Lady Di's engagement ring.

ment ring to Prince Charles drinking mugs, which sported handles in the shape of the heir-apparent's ear and Lady Di dolls.

The memorabilia marking the Royal Wedding generally fell into two categories: items officially produced by the British government and some twenty British Commonwealth member countries, and those brought into the market by private entrepreneurs. For a time it seemed that everyone from the British Post Office to novelty shops in New Jersey seemed determined to cash in on what was unquestionably *the* social event of the '80s.

Key among the "official" packages issued was an attractive glossy twelve-page booklet, printed by the British Post Office; its cover encased the 14-pence and 25-pence official wedding British postage stamps, released on July 22 and based on the engagement photos taken by the Earl of Snowdon. The book opens with a display of the coats of arms of the two families and includes brief biographical information about the couple. From there, the text breaks into a pitch for postage stamp collecting through an array of past monarchs who have appeared on British stamps. One page includes a photo of King George VI looking over his personal stamp album. The book ends by telling how to obtain "further details about British postage stamps and philatelic facilities" by writing to the Philatelic Bureau in Edinburgh. As it would turn out, it would be a banner year for Royal Wedding stamps.

Stamps

Stamps from the marriage of Prince Charles and Princess Diana have a special significance for stamp collectors, as they are the first Royal Wedding stamps ever issued for a (likely) future King and Queen of England. To appreciate the potential value of the two British stamps, one might take a look at how previous postage stamps commemorating royal

Prince Charles and Princess Diana engagement photo on stamps.

unions and their anniversaries have done over the years. The one-pound Silver Wedding commemorative for King George VI and Queen Elizabeth is worth in excess of $180, while the 1972 20-pence Silver Wedding commemorative for Queen Elizabeth II and Prince Philip has increased more than five times its original face value within ten years of its issue. The English stamps were just two of sixty-eight Royal Wedding Stamps issued by Commonwealth nations during 1981. Complete omnibus collections, including one of each of the sixty-eight stamps, were marketed by the British Royal Mint for $98.

Coins

The British also issued a coin—appropriately, a crown—to mark the wedding of Prince Charles and Princess Diana. The piece was a little larger than old American silver dollars and came in two variations: a silver proof designed specifically for sale to collectors, and a copper-nickel version produced for mass distribution to the public at its face value of 25 pence. The issuing of this coin also marked a first—the first time in its 1000-year history that the British Royal Mint issued a circulating coin for a Royal Wedding. It also is the first British coin to feature Prince Charles, and for that reason it is certain to increase in value when the Prince of Wales assumes the British throne, an event now expected to occur sometime after the turn of the next century.

No more than 250,000 of the silver proof Royal Wedding crowns were distributed, at a comparable cost of $65 each in U.S. currency. The mere limited-edition nature of the silver crowns will put them much more in demand in coming years than the copper-nickel version, which saw an estimated circulation of about 17 million. Even though this version was intended for general circulation, very few of the coins ended up among the daily pocket change of the British; due to its popularity, most of these coins were socked away as souvenirs. The Royal Mint also issued fifteen similar coins for Commonwealth countries, with versions turning up in places like the Ascension Islands, the Bahamas, Bermuda, and the Falkland Islands (which made its own history during the '80s).

American-Made Souvenirs

Obviously, there were no United States coins or stamps issued to commemorate the marriage of Prince Charles and his bride (for our part, President Reagan and the First Lady sent the couple an elliptical Steuben glass bowl valued at $8000 on behalf of the American people). But what we lacked in "official" commemoratives, we made up for in an avalanche of custom-made products. One American company, the Franklin Mint, issued no less than three items—a bone china plate, a goblet, and a sterling silver cameo—to mark the Royal union. The plate featured a floral arrangement designed by noted British botanical artist Mary Grierson and was crafted by Royal Doulton. The bouquet is framed with a border of royal blue, edged with twenty-two-karat gold trim. A cartouche bearing the monograms of the couple appears in the lower portion of the plate. Its 1981 issue price was $75. A bit more booty—$1950, in fact—was required to buy one of the 950 goblets that were produced. The goblet is identifiable by the three-feathers symbol from the coat of arms of the Prince of Wales incorporated into its stem. The pendant—produced in an edition of 35,750, and selling for $45 when new—bears a portrayal of the symbols of the British monarchy together with the individual symbols representing Charles and Diana, all set on a mirror background. Each pendant carries the words "Prince Charles and Lady Diana, 29 July 1981."

British Souvenirs

Dr. Swift of the Royalty Bookshop feels that the most collectable Royal Wedding memorabilia in the future will be "the items most closely associated with the ceremony." One example he cited is the official itinerary distributed to guests by Buckingham Palace, detailing the step-by-step agenda of events. "The Order of Procession, the Order of Service, and the Wedding Breakfast program from the day of the wedding provide a unique historical record of the events and their participants. These are rare, as they were only available to the major participants," he explained. Perhaps the most unusual official item Dr. Swift has heard of attaining collecting status is a piece of the Royal Wedding cake, which was given to one of the participants in the wedding and later found its way to the auction block, where it was used to raise money for the Falklands war effort. "This comes as close to a souvenir of the inside events as an outsider could get," he observed.

Another personal artifact is the Queen's 1981 Christmas card, which included an unpublished color photograph of the couple on its cover as, in Dr. Swift's words, "a symbolic recapitulation of the event of the year."

He also said that the higher-priced commercial items will almost certainly appreciate in value, such as the Gerrard & Co., Limited, "Royal Wedding Clock," marketed in 1981 for $1000 each. He said that collecting commemorative mugs is quite an undertaking in its own right, with over 100 different wedding mugs having been produced. "These mugs mostly represent the wedding," the doctor said, "but the few for the courtship are more rare."

Reading Matter—on Both Sides of the Atlantic

Dr. Swift said that printed material about the royal couple, and particularly about Princess Diana, was extremely popular both in the United States and the United Kingdom during the wedding year. "The American public went crazy buying books and magazines with the Princess on the cover," he said—a phenomenon that repeated itself during the couple's first visit together to this country in November 1985, when pictures of Princess Di could be found on no less than seven major American magazine covers during the week of the visit. "Any magazine with her on the cover had phenomenal increases in copies sold for that issue." For those whose interest was not satisfied by the sporadic burst of magazine covers during the decade, two new British periodicals hit the American market, supplying a constant diet for the starry-eyed royal-couple-watchers: *Majesty,* begun in November 1980, and *Royalty Monthly,* which debuted in June 1981. "They began to reach American consumers first through mail-order suppliers and then by appearing on the newsstands," Dr. Swift explained. Their large circulation numbers attest to the international popularity of Prince Charles and Princess Diana.

While the souvenirs marketed to celebrate the wedding were tastefully done for the most part, a few were downright silly. Dr. Swift said that among these items were cardboard cutouts of the Prince and Princess, which came with spring-mounted cardboard hands. These could be placed in the back seat of one's car "to make it look like they were waving from the window." The wedding bouquet had barely been tossed when marketeers were fast at work producing a line of Royal Baby items, most of which were humorous in nature. One example, which enjoyed a cross-over interest among paper doll collectors, was a cut-out book that hit the market in November 1983, *The Royal*

Royal Baby paper doll.

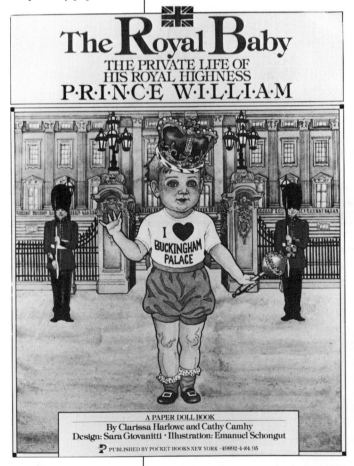

The **R**oyal **B**aby

THE PRIVATE LIFE OF
HIS ROYAL HIGHNESS
P·R·I·N·C·E W·I·L·L·I·A·M

A PAPER DOLL BOOK
By Clarissa Harlowe and Cathy Camhy
Design: Sara Giovanitti · Illustration: Emanuel Schongut
℗ PUBLISHED BY POCKET BOOKS NEW YORK · 49892-4·$4.95

Baby: The Private Life of His Royal Highness Prince William. Published by Pocket Books, with a text by Clarissa Harlowe and Cathy Camhy, its cover featured our boy Willie in caricature standing before the gates of the Royal Home. He is wearing a slightly oversized crown and an "I Love Buckingham Palace" T-shirt. The full-color book's original news release for the trade told us, "Prince William Arthur Philip Louis of Wales gained a worldwide following when he recently accompanied his royal parents on a trip to Australia and New Zealand, where the international press went wild as he stood, crawled, and smiled." Cut-out clothing in the book is designed to outfit the future William V for a day of sailing, playing polo, eating lunch (in a royal bib), or tracking wild game. Appropriate accessories include a cut-out copy of the "Magna Carta for Kids," a cut-glass baby bottle, and a beach outfit with pail and shovel for building (what else?) sand castles. The book retailed for $4.95, and copies have been turning up mid-decade for as much as $20.

The popularity of the Royal Family on these shores was emphasized when noted autograph specialist Charles Hamilton attempted to bring onto the market early in 1983 a group of letters that offered a personal glimpse into the life of the most-watched member of the Royal Family, Prince Charles. The letters, which were scheduled to be auctioned at Hamilton's New York gallery, were believed to be the first messages from a current resident of Buckingham Palace to reach the auction block. As it turned out, however, they never got that far. The four letters were written to one Anthony Craxton in the fall of 1976 and make reference to upcoming media exposure slated for the Prince. In one missive, the future King curses the incessant emphasis placed on his radio appearances, writing, "I have been persuaded to subject myself to yet another confrontation—with commercial radio. I still think it is a waste of time. I trust you are surviving the strain of all these preparations. Perhaps we shall end up in the same asylum next year when it is all over."

A torrent of British protest was accorded the news that Hamilton, known for bringing controversial pieces to auction from time to time, was going to open the letters for public bidding. In the end, Hamilton decided to withdraw the letters from the auction—but only after gaining a substantial amount of press coverage over the whole brouhaha.

Two World's Fairs

During the first half of the '80s, the United States was in the unique position of hosting two international world's fairs. However, the public for the most part decided to stay home; one fair turned out to be a marginal success, while the second was nothing short of a disaster. Yet in the grand scoreboard of collecting for the future, world's fairs do all right, regardless of their degree of commercial success at the time. In this century, the United States has hosted everything from the forgettable Golden Gate International Exposition to what many consider to have been the best American fair ever held, the New York World's Fair of 1939–40.

The Knoxville World's Fair of 1982 and the Louisiana World Exposition of 1984 were both sanctioned by the Bureau of International Expositions and were no more or less obscure than other BIE-sanctioned fairs of the '80s, such as the Munich exposition in 1983, which celebrated horticulture, a 1985 Japanese fair marking advances in science and technology in the

home, and Expo '86, held in Vancouver and honoring transportation.

World's fairs incorporate a wide range of specialists, according to Edward J. Orth of Exposition Collectors–Historians Organization (ECHO) (1436 Killarney, Los Angeles, CA 90065). "Some collect only one event, such as the Philadelphia Centennial of 1876 or Montreal's Expo 67," Orth explained. "Others collect specific items such as literature, postcards, stamps, medals, souvenirs, et cetera, from all or a group of fairs." ECHO lists 1285 members among its ranks, while another group of fair buffs, the World's Fair Collectors' Society, Inc. (148 Poplar St., Garden City, NY 11530), currently collects membership dues from 300 people yearly. Both clubs publish newsletters, where members monitor prices for past fair memorabilia and keep up to date on exposition activity around the globe.

Knoxville

Twenty-two members of ECHO list the Knoxville World's Fair of 1982 as their specialty. The Knoxville fair was the first time a southern American city hosted a sanctioned fair and the first world's fair held anywhere in the world since 1975. Fair organizers chose energy as the fair's theme, dramatized by a huge multi-glass solar ball called the Sunsphere, which hovered atop a six-story pedestal over the fair. It was designed to provide solar power to the United States Pavilion. Other similar exhibits were to be seen spread over the seventy-two-acre fair site situated in a part of town that had been a slum prior to its renovation for the fair. Unfortunately, the great energy awareness of the early '70s seems to have lost its avant-garde status in the '80s: the Knoxville fair may have had the misfortune of happening a decade too late. Nevertheless, the fair has left its mark via a considerable supply of items marketed during the run of the exposition. These include a grab bag of artifacts ranging from pop posters and gold coins to a particularly popular pocket watch. A series of four limited-edition posters by pop artist Peter Max, as well as a group of posters by noted Tennessean Howard Burger, were among the specific memorabilia showing up at the fair. A .999 percent gold commemorative coin and 1000 Tennessee Black Powder Rifle reproductions were also produced especially for the fair.

The 34th Knoxville World's Fair scrapbook.

For juvenile book collectors, two books resulted, *The Fun Book of World's Fairs* and *The Mystery of the World's Fair,* both of which were marketed at the fairgrounds.

Another book that came out of the Knoxville fair was an attractive scrapbook called *The 34th World's Fair Exposition,* featuring the photography of Jerry B. Reed printed in sepia tone, with brief background material provided by Knoxville bricklayer Clayton Cottrell. Published by Chrome Yellow Private Press of Gainesville, Florida, in September 1982, the book came in a slipcase and sold for $14.95. The first 1000 copies were autographed and numbered.

Novelty timepieces always enjoy a good track record as collectibles, and those coming out of the Knoxville exposition are no different. There were two models, both produced by Wagner Time, Inc., of Barrington, Illinois—a $99 mantel clock and a $21.95 pocket watch. The mantel clock measures 10 inches high and 6 inches wide, copying the classic lines of the famous Doric-Mosaic clock introduced by Elias Ingraham in 1880. It is made of mahogany, walnut, and polished brass. The clock operates on a quartz battery and each clock was individually numbered (at the bottom of the World's Fair logo). Westclox, a division of Gener-

Knoxville World's Fair mantle clock.

Timepiece from Knoxville World's Fair is a collectible to watch.

al Time Corp., manufactured the commemorative pocket watch, designed and sold by Wagner Time. World's fair collector Douglas P. Wollard of Bridgeton, Missouri, said that these are the sort of memorabilia he sees appreciating in value during the decade ahead. He pointed out that clocks from the Louisiana Purchase Exposition held in St. Louis in 1904 can bring $500 today.

Michael Pender of the World's Fair Collector's Society would agree with Wollard's assessment. During the summer of 1982, Pender appeared on ABC's "Good Morning America" anticipating the future worth of Knoxville items. At that time, he said that collectors and investors would be smart to single out the commemorative timepieces from the deluge of souvenirs. Focusing on the pocket watch in particular, which contains letters spelling out "Worlds Fair 82" in place of numbers around its face, as well as the fair's theme, "Energy Turns the World," Pender optimistically expressed the opinion that it might be like "the Mickey Mouse and Spiro Agnew watch someday."

Overshadowed by its energy theme was the fact that the

Knoxville World's Fair was the first American fair since 1904 in which the Peoples Republic of China participated. Consequently, artifacts gleaned from China's pavilion can be considered important remnants reflecting the international political climate between the two superpowers during the 1980s. The Soviet Union, by the way, did not attend. (This was only two years after the United States had boycotted the Moscow Olympics.)

Louisiana

The dust had barely settled on the Knoxville fair when a second southern exposition opened its gates. The Louisiana World Exposition ran from May 12 to November 11, 1984, during an oppressively hot summer that may have been largely responsible for the low turnout. Nevertheless, the fair, with its theme of "water on earth," resulted in a cavalcade of mementoes. In fact, the Louisiana fair had what must have been one of the most organized marketing departments ever accorded a modern-day fair. As early as 1981, everything from flags, T-shirts, tote bags to drinking glasses, jewelry, and posters were being cranked out, all bearing the official exposition

Louisiana World Exposition promotional booklets.

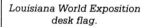

Louisiana World Exposition desk flag.

emblem: Robert Whitney's design of rhythmic white and silver lines over a blue circular field. The fair even had an official mascot, a top-hatted pelican given the impossible name of Seymore D. Fair.

The first two firms to receive licenses to produce posters for the fair were based in New Orleans, site of the exposition. A total of 4000 numbered and unsigned prints of Hugh Ricks' art nouveau–style lithograph showing a young woman holding the earth, being encircled by a ribbon of water, were marketed by ProCreations Publishing. A number of signed editions were distributed in limited quantities at selected galleries. The second poster, an allegorical drawing picturing mythical water gods, fish, and wildlife set amid a waterfall motif, was marketed by DKR Publishing, Inc. It was reproduced in a variety of mediums ranging from offset black-and-white prints, sold for $15 each, to a limited-edition steel engraving marketed for close to $300.

Much more common were the sales of the official fair souvenirs marketed by the exposition itself. These included lapel pins (sold in three varieties for from $2.25 to $3 each); gold and blue pendants ($2.75 and $3.50, respectively); a $5.50 tote bag; logo neckties in either navy or maroon ($12 each); and 4-by-6-inch desk flags (going for $2.75). T-shirts were marketed by four different firms, while the state of Louisiana issued 300,000 special world's fair license plates for motorists that year and the U. S. Postal Service released a postage stamp (joining previous series marking the New York fairs of 1939–40 and 1964, the Seattle fair of 1962, and the Knoxville fair). The U. S. Treasury produced 750,000 gold, silver, and bronze commemorative collectors' medallions. Even the

Miller Brewing Company tapped into a potential market by selling its product in special world's fair beer cans at the fairgrounds, as did Coca-Cola. The list goes on and on: pocketknives, ashtrays, cookbooks, letter openers, playing cards, cutting boards, belt buckles, raincoats, thermos bottles, caps, lighters, bookmarks...

A Comet Returns

"Do not open until the year 2062 A.D."

That's the note you'll want to attach to the next group of stuff. They're Halley's comet collectibles, circa 1985–86, and are guaranteed to be among the hottest collectibles to be had seventy-six years from now. The fact is, if your grandparents had left you a little nest egg of comet memorabilia dating from 1910, you might have been in the same enviable position Stuart Schneider and Roberta Etter found themselves in during the comet's most recent visit. The husband-and-wife collecting team were much in demand by magazine and newspaper interviewers throughout 1985, the year their book was published.*

*Halley's Comet, A 1910 Scrapbook, Abbeville Press.

Meanwhile, requests for reproduction rights for items in their collection arrived in their mail almost daily. All this because one day a few years ago Schneider and Etter set their scopes on becoming the country's leading authorities on Halley's comet collectibles.

They earned their recognition the hard way—by tracking Halley's Comet memorabilia from flea market to flea market all across the United States and Europe for six years. Stuart remembers how it all began: "The first thing we picked up was a sterling silver comet spoon," he told me. "Then we found a couple of comet postcards. It was then that we realized that here was an entire untapped collecting field. We decided to become comet experts." Thousands of dollars later, their Halley's collection is the foremost in the world.

While some items in the collection date from earlier visits by Halley's comet (the earliest item being a 1758 map showing the path of the comet across the heavens), the majority of artifacts date from the 1910 celestial rendezvous. Evidence of the comet's impact on fashion of the day can be seen in an ad run in the February 19, 1910, *Saturday Evening Post* unveiling men's

Mr. Halley's Comet guide by the editors of Sky & Telescope.

"comet collars." These were produced in two sizes, the "Halley's" and the "Comet." A great many of the comet-related products of 1910 found their market among people who actually believed that the coming of Halley's Comet spelled doom. It seems that a noted scientist of the time warned that the comet's tail contained cyanic gas, a component of cyanide. It was further explained that the earth was scheduled to pass through the comet's tail on May 18, 1910. "The fear was so real that a group of people actually went into a cave out West, equipped to wait out the passing of the comet's tail with the aid of oxygen cylinders," Schneider explained.

"Others bought comet umbrellas, which were protective devices designed to shield you from comet fallout." In fact, just about the only items to escape Schneider's grasp thus far are comet pills. "I've read about them in newspaper accounts of the time," he said, "but I've never seen any." The pellets, which were reportedly nothing more than sugar pills, were sold for a dollar a bottle to the fearful and gullible in 1910. They offered "guaranteed safety" from the poisonous fumes of Halley's Comet.

Not everyone took such an ominous view of the comet's 1910 return. At the time of the comet's closest approach, all sorts of parties and celebrations flourished, including one reported by *The New York Times* taking place at the home of Miss Gertrude T. Cruser of Flatbush. "All wore black robes and masks," the paper reported. "The parlors were decked out with imitation spiders and their webs. At the time of the rising of the comet, all those present adjourned to the rear veranda, where they tried to find it in the skies with telescopes." Today Schneider is the happy owner of a comet party hat, as well as all sorts of 1910 paper ephemera, all of which steadily increased in value as the

1986 visit approached. Good clean comet postcards, which only ten years ago could hardly fetch $5, sold for between $20 and $40 each throughout 1986. Searching intensified to such a degree that by the time the average person heard about the soaring sums to be had for 1910 comet collectibles, there was hardly a one to be found on flea market tables. Early bird collectors had grabbed them all up.

While 1910 comet items are now hard to come by, souvenirs of the 1986 visit are ripe for the picking. Relegated to yard-sale status, as is often the case with booms after the bubble has burst, their value

Comet paraphernalia.

R Tokens In 1910 some sincere—if misguided—souls prophesied all sorts of doomsday scenarios for the comet's approach and some charlatans even sold "comet insurance." Humorously contrasting with the more sophisticated and skeptical attitudes of the 80's are these "wooden nickels" inscribed in remembrance of the 1985-86 return. Set of three.
Tokens **$1.25**

Q Commemorative Medals Sure to be a collector's item, the Halley's Comet Commemorative Medal designed and engraved at the respected Roger Williams Mint, depicts Sir Edmond Halley and the dates of the Comet's appearances. The reverse, inspired by the historical fear

P Pins A bit less than an inch in diameter, the Cloisonné enamel Comet pin depicts a stylized comet with a brilliant red and yellow tail extending beyond the perimeter of the deep blue background. Limited edition. Available in tack (pictured) or stick pin.
P1 Tack
P2 Stick
Pins . . . . **$6.95 ea.**

of the comet, shows it stylized as a monster dashing toward Earth. Comes in protective plastic case. Available in bronze (pictured—Q1) or sterling silver (Q2).
Q1 Bronze . . . . **$15.00 ea.**
Q2 Silver . . . . **$40.00 ea.**

will gradually increase each year between now and the time of Halley's next visit to our part of the solar system in 2062. You can be the hero to your great-grandchildren by scouting up some of the items marketed during this decade by companies like Halley's Comet Watch '86/General Comet Industries, Inc. For four years prior to the return of the comet, this New Jersey—based company was busy developing and franchising comet collectibles ranging from bumper stickers selling for $1.25 each (one reads "Repent! Halley's Comet is Coming") to a $199 telescope called the Halleyscope. Company founder Owen Ryan, who together with friends sank $200,000 into his venture, was quoted in 1985 as expecting to gross $10 million from his products—not including the Halleyscope. The company left nothing to chance, branching out with subsidiaries into Canada, western Europe, and what Ryan called "comet-crazy" Japan. A two-minute commercial for the Halleyscope was produced and an aggressive direct mail catalog campaign began in 1985. Asked at a press conference why the average person cares about all this anyway, Ryan's retort was that Hal-

ley's Comet is just too grand to be ignored.

This sentiment was shared by others who comprised the flourishing comet cottage industry of the mid-'80s. A company called Halcom (short for Halley's Comet Marketing Associates) made plans to sell seven million bronze medallions bearing a phrase that translates from Latin as "Save us from the evil of the comet" at $12 a pop. Silver and gold versions were also available. Hallmark supplied its card shops with a jigsaw puzzle picturing a cluster of vintage comet memorabilia taken from the Schneider collection, while over thirty comet books were being marketed in 1985. Meanwhile, *USA Today* reported, six months before the comet first became vaguely visible to the naked eye, that two Albuquerque air traffic controllers, Larry Lawton and Wayne Hicks, had already sold 75,000 comet T-shirts, caps, and sheets of stickers. "People always want to pick up a memento of a show they've been to," Lawton was quoted as saying. "Well, this is going to be one great show."

For those of us on earth, Lawton's remark now appears to have been over optimistic. Great show or not, the return of Halley's Comet was a once-in-a-lifetime occurrence, and the comet fallout will be turning up for decades—all of which will find their stock reaching maturity in the year 2062. If you are considering filling a trunk with 1986 comet souvenirs for your descendants' fun and profit, comet buff Stuart Schneider suggests that you are best off to consider those items that are made "with love for Halley's Comet, rather than those that are likely to be produced by people merely desiring to catch a fast buck." That is, of course, unless you happen across some comet pills.

3. Pieces of History

The first time I ever saw what might be called an honest-to-goodness piece of history in marketable form was when I was a teenager. I was helping some friends clean out a storage closet at the local VFW hall where a rummage sale was about to be held. (Some kids hung around the malt shops; I hung around rummage sales.) In what looked like the proverbial closet of Fibber McGee, my friends and I came across a time-yellowed 8″ x 10″ piece of cardboard with some turn-of-the-century lithography on it. Attached to the middle of the card was a small sliver of wood. The lithography included a reproduction of the signers of the Constitution gathered in Independence Hall. The accompanying information on the card explained that this crumbling splinter was "an actual piece of the floorboard removed from Independence Hall," the very same floor over which our founding fathers had walked. The flooring had been removed during a renovation and some farsighted junk man, who sensed a souvenir in the making, had backed a wagon up to the door.

Items associated with important historical moments, places, or people have long been the object of public fascination. In the religious world, they are called "relics." The most famous of these, no doubt, is the miraculously preserved hand of St. Francis Xavier, which has been credited with performing all sorts of miracles down through the centuries. Important objects, and religious relics in particular, have been said to possess a certain aura. I got a spooky feeling myself when I touched Charles Dickens's coat while visiting the P. T. Barnum museum in Bridgeport, Connecticut.

Souvenirs from Outer Space

If Phineas Barnum were alive today, he would no doubt be wowing audiences with objects associated with the manned space program. But as the great showman is long gone, the torch has been passed to others—people like Michael Noble. In 1982, Noble, of Cupertino, California, garnered national press attention when he began marketing half-inch slices of Space Shuttle tile. Noble had obtained a few sheets of the actual tile used in the first Shuttle from his father just before NASA clamped a lid on public use of the material. Michael's father, Douglas, worked at the plant where the tile was made and had planned to line his fireplace with the material, which is made to withstand temperatures in excess of 2000 degrees Fahrenheit. Michael, however, saw a marketing opportunity. He had the sheets cut into small triangular wafers and had each one packaged in foil-stamped plastic cases. Called "A Collector's Issue Honoring the U.S. Space Shuttle" and retailing for $7.75, Noble's tile packages hit the market just at the right moment—riding on the coattails of international news coverage of the first successful Shuttle mission. The cash register first began ringing when he set up a tent shop near the Shuttle landing runway at Edwards Air Force base the day the spacecraft was first tested in July 1982.

Shortly after that, Noble began marketing his souvenirs to shops far beyond his California home. Shuttle tiles were enjoying brisk sales not only in shops in the United States, but in Europe and Japan as well.

Space Shuttle T-shirt.

Closer to home, Dixie Quinlin, who runs a business called Star Base Central in Mountain View, California, quickly sold out of the two dozen packets she bought from Noble's firm, which she said were swept up by people who buy anything dealing with the Space Shuttle. Noble would readily admit that he counts himself among the '80s small but dedicated band of space buffs. "The space program and the Shuttle program are one of the greatest achievements of mankind, comparable to Columbus's discoveries," Noble said at the time in unabashed enthusiasm. His tiles, he said, allowed people to "buy a small piece of America."

Space Shuttle tile marketed by California man.

I didn't hear much about Noble after the initial burst of press coverage. Consequently, in the summer of 1985 I wrote to his company, at the address listed on the back of the Space Shuttle tiles, to find out how many tiles he had ultimately sold. My letter came back stamped ''Return To Sender.'' It's a safe guess that Noble had tapped a vein that is now exhausted. But his story points up the short-lived availability of some of these ''pieces of history.'' The rule of thumb is: if you want to add it to your collection, mail your check off before midnight tonight. It may not be there next week.

Outer space again found its place into the world of entrepreneurship when an outfit called PSEnterprises of Pittsburgh, presided over by Patsy Samson, came out of the blue with three items that seemed too unbelievable to be true. But authentic they are, and she has a letter from NASA to prove it. Samson's products: paperweights and a poster containing actual fragments of America's first space station, Skylab, which fell to earth on July 11, 1979, after it was abandoned by NASA. While these objects preserve pieces of 1970s (rather than '80s) history, the paperweights come under our observation here because they didn't appear on the collectibles market until 1984.

I first met up with Patsy Samson, a former interior decorator, at a limited-edition show at the Nassau Coliseum on Long Island in May of 1984. It was in this unlikely environment of Norman Rockwell figurines and collector plates featuring children in fields of daisies that Samson had taken a booth to market her pieces of Skylab. I asked her whether this was the same Skylab that a few years earlier had been the object of an international scramble to guess where it might fall. She said it was, graciously pointing out that NASA had put only one Skylab station into orbit. And now pieces of it could be found in little clear spheres and prisms here in the Nassau Coliseum. How?

Samson's story dates back to the day a friend called her in 1983 to tell her about a Mr. Norton in the remote back country of Australia, where Skylab crash-landed, who wanted to sell a one-ton chunk he had found. Seeing an opportunity, Samson contacted the Australian and purchased what turned out to be the fiberglass and metal remains of one of the spacecraft's oxygen tanks. What resulted, in fact, were three products: a Correia art glass globe with a piece of Skylab appearing suspended over a miniature earth, a Lucite pyramid also with a piece encased in it, and a limited-edition poster with a fragment attached to its surface.

Along with the purchase from Norton and an agreement to share future royalties with him came a copy of a letter of authentication dated November 26, 1979, which the man from Down Under had received from NASA's George C. Marshall Space Flight Center in Alabama, verifying that this was in fact Skylab "reentry de-

Pyramid paperweight containing actual piece of Skylab.

bris." To add further to the authenticity, Samson secured a letter written by Charles "Pete" Conrad, Jr., one of the three astronauts who took part in the first Skylab mission in May 1973. In the letter, a copy of which is marketed with each of Samson's products, the former astronaut said, "I was extremely proud to have been a part of this program and especially fortunate to have been a member of the first crew to occupy Skylab. This fragment is certainly symbolic of our first 'Space

Station' accomplishment.'' Samson took her products on the road in '83, approaching the Smithsonian, Walt Disney World, and Epcot Center, as well as various space museums and planetariums across the country, as potential sales outlets. The fastest selling of the three items was the 17-by-22-inch poster priced at $25. The pyramid sold for $65, while the top of the line item was the Correia glass, which came in its own custom-designed walnut case and cost $250.

In 1985, I contacted Samson again and found that she was still very actively marketing her Skylab pieces. "You know, I was told by NASA that this is the first time that the American public has had a chance to buy something that's been in outer space," Samson explained. The public's reaction to her products since their debut has been "fantastic," Samson said. "People are absolutely fascinated with the fact that it actually was in outer space, and also the fact that it's part of America's first and only space station. It's like owning a piece of the Kitty Hawk." I asked her how sales of the fast-selling poster were going; she explained, "We did an initial run of just over 5000 posters and they are now all

Piece of Skylab, encased in Correia glass.

gone. I decided that after we sold out the posters, we would come back with an upgraded product to replace it." She said she acquired a film negative of Skylab from NASA and is now marketing 16-by-20-inch photographs of the space station with a piece of Skylab attached to it. "The picture shows Skylab as taken by Skylab's final crew," she said. "The quality is exceptional." It retails for $29.95.

Samson is presently concentrating on her most ambitious venture yet. "I am in the process of negotiating with Correia to do another Skylab limited-edition paperweight—we are working on the prototype now—which is going to knock the socks off the market." She is receiving help with her new creation from a friend in the electronic furniture business. "We are going to produce an electronic box which opens by remote control." The moment it opens, "a light goes on inside and you see what is in the piece of Correia. It's going to be incredible."

A Street Paved with Opportunity

While Noble and Samson had their heads turned skyward in search of hot collectibles during the decade, two brothers in Chicago had to look no further than right under their feet to find a business opportunity. Their success adds some credence to the saying that the streets of America are paved with gold—all you need is a jackhammer. History has it that Chicago's State Street—the same one Frank Sinatra sang about as being "that great street"—was the first portion of the town to be rebuilt after Mrs. O'Leary's cow knocked over that famous kerosene lantern in October 1871, resulting in a major portion of downtown Chicago burning to the ground. A century after the rebuilding, Windy City officials decided to excavate a

State Street paperweight.

portion of the street to make way for what today is the State Street Mall. Enter Robert and Michael Proko. Hearing about the dismantling going on at a part of one of the world's most famous boulevards, the brothers rushed to the scene with a van and secured a seventeen-pound granite block. Before a year was out, they were selling small chips of the block through an outfit called, appropriately enough, The Great Street Emporium. Each piece was encased in leaded glass and marketed as a paperweight. Affixed to the base of each paperweight was a sepia-tone print of State Street as it looked in 1913.

The paperweights sold for $19.95 apiece, with the largest number marketed through advertisements in the *Chicago Sun-Times* and a well-placed display in a leading Chicago bookstore in the summer of 1982. Within six months, the brothers had sold over 2000 of their curios. The Prokos expected to have depleted their stock within the year, but are making plans to reprise their paperweights a few years from now. They saved the first 999 for themselves and, if all goes as expected, plan to sell them at the Chicago World's Fair in 1992.

A Bridge Across Time

While the Prokos were selling pieces of State Street encased in glass, half a continent away a retired restaurateur named Robert Smith was watching the profits roll in from the 200 tons of original Golden Gate Bridge cable wire he purchased during the renovation of the famous span in 1975. Smith (whose business cards identify him as "A Smith Called Bob") remembers walking across the 8981-foot bridge on the day it first opened, May 27, 1937; he was twelve years old at the time. One night not long after, he and a friend climbed up the bridge's cable to its top towers, armed only with a flashlight. He'll tell you, however, that his best memory of the bridge remains the day he

San Francisco cable car rail.

Golden Gate Bridge cable.

returned from duty during World War II along with other homecoming veterans. Their ship entered San Francisco Bay and passed right under the Golden Gate Bridge.

During the '80s, Smith was selling three-pound chunks of cable from the bridge he loves for $12.95. Cut to 3-inch lengths, the tightly wrapped pieces (made of 85 percent carbide steel) were painted orange and delivered along with a wooden display stand and a certificate of authenticity. Thousands have been sold. As a result of this initial success, Smith returned with gift boxes containing "Genuine San Francisco Cable Car Rail." He explained in a small note packed in each box that the pieces were cut from a section of sixty-pound T rail he acquired as a result of the shutdown and rebuilding of the city's cable car system in September 1982. As San Francisco's cable car system debuted with a foggy, predawn run on the morning of August 2, 1873, Smith's souvenirs carry the dates 1873 and 1982.

A Sign of the Times

A landmark of a decidedly different nature is the H-O-L-L-Y-W-O-O-D sign, which looks down over Tinseltown from the Hollywood Hills. The sign stands five stories high and covers more ground than a football field. Erected in 1923, of tin coated with white paint, it has served as a beacon to the starry-eyed multitudes who have flocked to Hollywood in search of a career in the movies, symbolizing both the glamour and the shattered dreams that are part of the film capital's legend. (Stage actress Peg Entwistle jumped to her death from the letter "H" in 1932.) The sign originally read "Hollywoodland"; the letters L-A-N-D were taken down in 1949.

You may think that the sign that continues to wow tourists today is the same one that has been there all these years, but not so. In 1980, Hank Berger, a promotional entre-

Pieces of the Hollywood sign came attractively displayed.

preneur and Hollywood buff from Sun Valley, California, bought the original sign after it had been replaced with an identical one. Berger's game plan was to market small cut-up squares of the sign as souvenirs— 30,000 pieces sold for $29.95 each. While Berger admittedly made some money through his enterprise, he said that he did it basically to attract attention to his budding promotion business. And for three years, the sign did just that. After presenting complimentary pieces to Presidents Carter and Reagan, as well as to Frank Sinatra, Berger found himself the subject of a feature story in *People* magazine, and as a much-in-demand guest on television talk shows

41

in this country and Europe.

When I last heard of Berger, he was trying to unload the remaining portion of the sign; the 30,000 1 1/4-inch squares he had sold hardly made a dent in the supply of gigantic letters. His asking price was $175,000, or about $19,000 per letter. Berger pointed out that the remaining letters, which weighed in at four tons and were cut and stacked in 3-by-9-foot sheets, could produce two million more souvenirs. You'll have to pick them up with your own truck, however.

A Ticket to the Past

A popular expression found in many collectibles advertisements during the '80s is "warehouse find"—items uncovered in mint condition, said to have reposed unnoticed for years in some murky corner of a storage building. And when it comes to warehouse finds, Harvey Fishman hit the jackpot the day he discovered 10,000 unused tickets to the greatest rock music event of the 1960s: Woodstock. It was back in the summer of 1969 that 400,000 people converged on an upstate New York town for what was officially titled the Woodstock Music and Art Fair. Somehow the art end of the event got lost in what would be remembered as the archetypal outdoor rock concert. Thousands of tickets were printed in advance for the event, but as crowds began arriving in greater numbers than had been anticipated, and gate-crashing ran rampant, organizers threw in the towel and let everyone in for free. The tickets that were not distributed that weekend remained stored for thirteen years at the Globe Ticket Company's warehouse in Boston, until Fishman, a creative director with a New York advertising agency, realized their marketability and bought them for an undisclosed amount. Fishman began marketing the paper pieces of rock history through his company, Investment Galleries of New York. For $24 (the original price of the three-day pass), plus $6 handling, you received an actual green combination ticket bearing the dates August 15, 16, and 17, 1969. As an added touch, each ticket was placed inside a Lucite case with a black paper liner. "Now! The '60s Can Live Forever," ads for the tickets announced. Tickets would be sold on a "first-come-first-served basis," the sales pitch went on to say. "Even their obvious investment potential is overshadowed by their very personal social, cultural and nostalgic significance to all of us who lived through America's tumultuous sixties." Ironically, many of the tickets were ultimately purchased by young people who were toddlers during the Woodstock generation years.

Cut from the Deck

One day in 1983 I received a phone call from a gentleman named Jim Howell of Broken Arrow, Oklahoma. He was eager to tell me about a business opportunity that had dropped into his lap. It seemed that Howell had acquired an authentic piece of nautical history, the schooner *Atlantic*, which found a place in history books in 1905 when the Kaiser of Germany, looking to test his skills, sponsored a transatlan-

Plaque mounted on piece of deck from the schooner Atlantic.

tic sailboat race. The 185-foot topsail schooner, built and owned by Listerine mouthwash magnate William Marshall, raced away with a world's record for a single-hulled craft, making the distance from New York to England in twelve days, four hours, and nineteen minutes, piloted by Captain Charlie Barr. The *Atlantic*'s record holds to this very day.

Built just before the race, the *Atlantic* went on to a colorful career in racing, until yachting events fell on hard times during the '30s. The boat was brought out of retirement during the war, serving as a mine sweeper and submarine tender, only to be relegated to a floating gift shop in the '50s. The craft literally sank into oblivion off the coast of Norfolk, Virginia. The Metro Machine Company of Norfolk, located off the waters where the schooner went down, needed dock space and hauled the wreck in and had it dismantled. A portion of the mast and deck was donated to the city of Norfolk. Howell, who had long expressed an interest in the *Atlantic* (and at one time envisioned raising the craft and restoring it to its original seafaring condition), was called and asked if he wanted the remaining portion of the deck. He did. Howell had his share of the teak deck cut into 2 3/4-by-5-inch pieces and, mounting them to a descriptive pewter plaque, began marketing them for $15 each. The raised pewter plaque testifies that the attached piece of wood is an "original piece of deck from the schooner *Atlantic*—Fastest sailing yacht ever built." It was Howell's hope to market 10,000 pieces of the craft before depleting his stock.

Future Dreams, Future Treasures

The merits of jackhammering or taking a blowtorch to historic landmarks for ultimate monetary gain can be debated for hours. There are those who fear that such a practice will ultimately allow national treasures to fall into the hands of such marketeers. One might wonder if it is only a matter of time before we'll be seeing pieces of the Declaration of Independence and Grant's Tomb turning up inside paperweights. It might therefore be appropriate to point out that nearly all the items that have come into the hands of collectibles merchants had already been destined for the trash heap. This is not to say that such concern is not without its merits. Even

as these words are being written, there are many golddiggers dreaming of salvaging the recently discovered *Titanic*. Some may simply want to add a piece of the legendary ship to their collections, but a much bigger lure has been the rumored million dollars in jewelry contained in the ship's purser's safe. These untold riches have been part of the attraction to Texas oilman Jack Grimm. Grimm funded three search expeditions to find the ship before a joint U.S.-French team announced that they had found it, about 560 miles off Newfoundland. For his part, Grimm was quoted in *USA Today* as saying that the *Titanic* was his because he had pinpointed the ship's location as early as 1981. He vowed to launch a salvage expedition. "We don't intend to raise it," he said. "We'll film it and recover some of the valuables." The U.S.-French team expressed the opinion that tampering with the ship would be tantamount to "the desecration of this memorial to 1500 souls" who went down with the *Titanic* in 1912. Meanwhile, a London insurance company, Commercial Union, staked a claim on the ship, saying that it is the descendant of a group of companies that insured the *Titan-*

ic before its maiden voyage and paid out $1.4 million in compensation after the disaster. In late 1985, a Welshman made news by announcing his intention to raise the *Titanic* wreckage by the use of hydrogen-filled canvas bags.

While parties battling it out over salvage rights to the *Titanic* first made international headlines during the second half of 1985, a small news blip hit the wire services, noting that a company called the Big Apple Land Corporation was selling deeds to square inches of property in Manhattan for $5 each. You received with your purchase an official deed identifying you as a landowner in the world's most expensive real estate market. The whole thing was offered just for fun and is an idea that has been around for a while. Perhaps the most famous real estate venture of this kind happened during the 1950s, when 21 million kids acquired land in the Klondike after it was offered as a premium during the "Sgt. Preston of the Yukon" television program. The Klondike Big Inch Land premium was the most successful promotional gimmick Quaker Oats came up with during its years of sponsoring the Preston radio and TV series. The deeds were given away in boxes of Quaker Puffed Wheat and Quaker Puffed Rice in 1955, granting the holder ownership of one square inch of land in Canada's Yukon Territory. The company actually purchased eighteen acres of what was basically scrub land twelve miles north of Dawson. Quaker Oats formed The Klondike Big Inch Land Company, Inc., and divided up the property into 21 million square-inch lots. The giveaway was hugely successful for the company, despite the fact that the deeds were in reality worthless to the deedholder, as the Canadian government retained all mineral rights to the land and the Klondike Big Inch Land Company has long since gone out of existence. But the deeds, dating back more than thirty years now, are much in demand among collectors, selling for as high as $40 at collector shows.

Armchair Property-Owning in Space

Missed out on the great Yukon land deal? Fear not, things are looking up for claim stakers during the '80s. In 1983, a Santa Maria, California, outfit called Extraterrestrial Estates offered land for sale on the planet Mars. Folks who sent the company $15.95

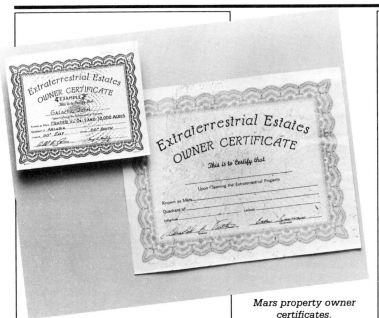

Mars property owner certificates.

received a small topographic map, a snapshot of the "property" (a NASA picture taken on the Martian surface during the unmanned Viking mission), and a deed. If your vacation plans run closer home, the people at Boston's Museum of Science were able to set you up with a nice piece of property on the Moon during a fund-raising effort in 1985. Prices ranged from $25 for a rather unspectacular crater lot to $1000 in the Sea of Tranquillity, which gained so much attention during the Apollo 11 mission. "Neil Armstrong walked on it," the real estate brochure said. "Now you can own it." All property was guaranteed to be on the sunny side of the moon with a full view of the Earth's surface.

Remember the Volcano

You don't have to go to the Moon, however, to reap profits from a crater. Just ask Marti Studhalter of Morton, Washington. She has found a way to turn volcanic ash into cold hard cash. Martha "Marti" Studhalter and her husband, Richard, have lived in Morton for fifty years and to hear them tell it, not much happened in this small logging community (pop. 1200) until the morning of May 18, 1980. It was then that Mount St. Helens, an 8364-foot volcano, blew its top, letting loose with a force as powerful as 500 atomic bombs. The Studhalters, who live twenty-one air miles from the mountain, were at home at the time. "The house shook from the big blast," Mr. Studhalter recalled. "The big ash cloud came over and started to fall. Everything turned black and the street lights went on." After the dust cleared, the couple found their yard covered with three inches of volcanic ash.

Today Marti makes ceramics out of the ash she and her husband have collected from all over the state of Washing-

ton in the wake of the original eruption. Having been a certified ceramics teacher for seventeen years, Marti used to spend her time teaching. Since Mount St. Helens came into her life, she doesn't have time to teach. "We can hardly keep up with the demand," Mr. Studhalter said. When not giving tours through her minifactory ("It's getting to be quite a tourist attraction"), Mrs. Studhalter can be found working feverishly with one of the 3000 different molds she uses to create her Mount St. Helens Ash Creations, producing everything from small vases, bells, and animal figurines to large pitchers and bowls. "The reaction to these pieces has been tremendous," Mr. Studhalter said. As near as the couple could estimate,

Mt. St. Helen's ash ceramic box, bell and cougar.

Mt. St. Helen's vase and mug made by Marti's Ceramics.

they've sold about 10,000 conversation pieces made from the most famous volcano in American history. In fact, Marti says she has to fire sixty to seventy pieces a day just to keep up with the demand. "They're now scattered all over the United States and overseas," Mr. Studhalter said.

What acccounts for the fabulous reception accorded the products of this one-woman assembly line? "It's because they come from the mountain," Marti explained. "People go up and see the volcano and want to take a little bit of the mountain home with them." Has business diminished at all in the years since Mount St. Helens was front-page news? "If anything, it has increased," Mrs. Studhalter said. "Surprisingly, business was real slow at first. People were afraid of the mountain and they didn't want to get anywhere near it." The settling down of the volcano and the building of a brand new blacktop highway, allowing for a steady stream of tourists to get up close to the volcano, have turned things around. "We now get busloads of people stopping by," Marti said.

4. Anniversaries

The Brooklyn Bridge

"Millions of spectators thronged into lower Manhattan last night for the biggest bash in New York history," the *New York Post* reported on May 25, 1983. "On land, sea and in the air, they hailed the centennial for the mightiest span of them all—the beautiful Brooklyn Bridge."

When the Brooklyn Bridge marked its one hundredth anniversary in 1983, it was a gala affair of the sort only the Big Apple could muster. Rededication Day, as the actual anniversary date was called, saw the biggest flotilla of harbor craft since the Bicentennial in 1976. A 200-pound birthday cake in the shape of (you guessed it) the bridge had been baked. There was a two-and-a-half-hour parade, while horns and whistles and cannons blared all along the East River. That night, the skies over Manhattan were aglow with $150,000 worth of fireworks launched from the bridge's twin towers. "This was New York at its best," Mayor Ed Koch told the press.

When the skies cleared and the day had passed into the history books, New Yorkers

New York Post *edition for the Brooklyn Bridge centennial.*

had more than memories to remember the day by—lots more. The selling of the Brooklyn Bridge was big business in 1983. A company called the Bridgestone Corporation of New York was one of a handful of companies selling actual pieces of the Brooklyn Bridge as souvenirs—fulfilling one of New York City's alltime favorite gaglines. What was actually being sold were 2 1/2-by 2-by-1/4-inch pieces of the bridge's anchorage granite, yours for only $14.95, plus $2 postage and handling—major credit cards accepted. Each stone carried a "diamond-engraved" black-and-bronze plaque and came packaged in a gift box bearing the official

48

seal of the Brooklyn Bridge Centennial Commission. "This granite is more than a rock," promotional advertising for the pieces of the bridge announced. "It represents a significant part of our proud history. It's as important as Betsy Ross' flag, the golden spike linking the Transcontinental Railroad, or even a hunk of moon rock." Even as Bridgestone was grabbing attention with its granite, other official licensees were marketing pieces of the actual cable wire from the bridge encased in Lucite, as well as slivers of the recently replaced original wooden pedestrian walkway.

While these types of items were obviously limited by virtue of their very nature, there were plenty of Brooklyn Bridge commemoratives to go around for anyone who wanted them. At the high end of the scale were diamond-studded, gold-plated bridge pins priced at $2000 apiece. Heavy bucks were also being paid for original silk-screened commemorative posters by Andy Warhol, which sold in excess of $1500. Pewter cigarette boxes with reproductions of the opening day invitations were being marketed for $75, and glass paperweights, with the same invitation, were priced at between $12 and

Brooklyn Bridge centennial poster issued in conjunction with book.

$30. A spokesman for Hamilton Projects, which served as the licensed merchandiser for the centennial, was quoted in 1983 as predicting that, all totaled, sales of officially licensed products marketed as a result of the bridge's birthday would top $30 million, twice what it cost to build the bridge in the first place.

Anniversaries have an effect on vintage memorabilia much like the stock market. As an anniversary approaches, collector/speculators go into action. I witnessed an example of this phenomenon in practice at an ephemera show

Mary J. Shapiro
A PICTURE HISTORY OF
THE BROOKLYN BRIDGE
Dover Publications, Inc., New York

in Rye, New York, early in 1981. A couple were systematically going up and down either side of the booth aisles asking dealers, "What do you have on the Brooklyn Bridge?" I watched them pay out ready cash for everything from ashtrays and postcards to scarves, books, and song sheets bearing the image of the famous span. The prices were still stable, and my guess is they spent a couple of hundred dollars that day. This was the first time I became aware of the impending Brooklyn Bridge market about to explode on the collectibles world. A few weeks later I was at another collecting show, this time in Boston, and I came across a diamond-shaped trade card showing the bridge as it looked in the 1880s, printed about that time by Clark's Spool Cotton. I paid $7 for it. Two years later, at the height of Brooklyn Bridge mania, cards just like mine were selling for $30. I figured that, based on this, that couple I saw in Rye had cashed in their bridge chips in May 1983 for a comparable across-the-board increase.

The Statue of Liberty

Anniversaries have been responsible, to a good degree, for helping establish some of the biggest prices attained at auction by vintage memorabilia during the decade. The approaching centennial of the Statue of Liberty certainly was on the minds of those gathered in the Sotheby's New York auction gallery in April 1982 when a late nineteenth-century weathervane, modeled after the Statue of Liberty, came up for bids. Made by the J. L. Mott Iron Works of New York and Chicago, the molded and gilded copper artifact set a world's record for a vane when a New York collector purchased it for $75,000. Vintage models of Miss Liberty, originally produced to raise money to build the famous 302-foot-high statue and to install its base in New York, toppled all records when they hit the auction block at Christie's in New York in 1985. In reporting on the auction, *The New York Times* said, "With the centennial celebration of the statue's installation scheduled for the Fourth of July next year, the pace is quickening in sales of vintage versions of what is Frédéric Auguste Bartholdi's greatest sculpture." At the auction, three metal copies of what was at first known as "Liberty Enlightening the World" were offered; the largest of the trio netted $121,000.

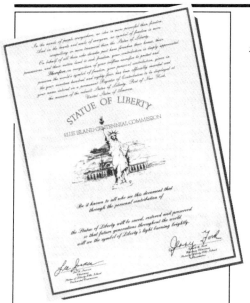

It was purchased by the chairman of the Coca-Cola Bottling Company of New York. A spokesman said that Coke's interest centered around the centennial. Two other Statue of Liberty models, a French-made 3-foot-tall version and an American-made model measuring 38 inches in height, were both purchased by noted Statue of Liberty collector William Gaines. Gaines, who is the publisher of *Mad* magazine, paid a total of $42,900 for the pair. The statues were slated to join his collection of 200 other Statues of Liberty that Gaines and Anne P. Griffiths have on display throughout their Manhattan apartment. Speaking about the appeal of the Statue of Liberty,

Gaines told the *Times*, "Most people think that the Statue of Liberty is not a great piece of art. I couldn't care less. We just love it for what it is." This love has not stopped Gaines from occasionally poking fun at the lady with the torch via the pages of *Mad*, including a cartoon the magazine recently ran showing a helicopter hovering near the ear of the statue—cleaning it with a huge cotton swab.

While discussion of refurbishing the Statue of Liberty has been a topic of conversation for years, it was the approaching centennial that provided the impetus to set things in motion. To do so, the American public was once again asked to dig down deep into its pockets. But instead of employing scale models to entice contributions, as was the case a century ago, appeals came in the form of printout letters from none other than Lee Iacocca, the savior of the Chrysler Corporation. Iacocca was chosen by President Reagan to serve as chairman of The Statue of Liberty/Ellis Island Foundation, Inc., in 1982. I received my note from Mr. Iacocca (as did millions of others on the various mailing lists the foundation used to make its pitch) one day in 1983. Even though I have never met Mr.

Statue of Liberty scale models sold during statue's centennial.

Iacocca nor owned a Chrysler, he began his missive with "Dear Friend," and went on to tell me that "a century of exposure to the corrosive salt air" has not only resulted in considerable exterior deterioration to the great statue in New York Harbor, but "severely damaged the internal structure of the Statue as well." It was going to cost $25 million to restore the statue to its original beauty. If I sent a donation, my name would be listed in the Statue of Liberty Register of Contributers. "As part of the Centennial Celebration, this historic register will be officially entered in the archives of the Statue of Liberty National Monument Museum where it will be on permanent display," Iacocca promised in the printout. And that's not all. For making a donation, I'd receive a "unique certificate" acknowledging the fact. Who said vanity never works? Not only did the foundation raise the needed funding to meet its July 4, 1986, deadline largely through this successful drive, but it distributed a great number of the donation certificates to boot—coveted personal souvenirs of the Statue of Liberty's one-hundredth-birthday party.

Now enter the hoopla. In anticipation of the statue's centennial, American ingenuity went into high gear. As with no other anniversary to date, opportunists, both official and unofficial, seemed determined to outdo each other to create the ultimate '80s memento commemorating the world's most photographed statue. There were the usual items: first day covers, collector plates, souvenir books by the scores, and reproductions of old prints. (One leading New York shop, "Welcome to New York City," reported selling thousands of $5 repros of a "projected drawing" of the Statue of Liberty published in *Harper's* in 1875.) Among the more ingenious products were scale models marketed by TMX International, Inc., dealers in gold, silver, and platinum bullion. TMX used the original Bartholdi mold to create an edition of 100 numbered pure silver sculptures of the statue. Their special hook was the fact that the statues were being produced in France by the same firm, N. Arthur Bertrand Co., that worked closely with Bartholdi in the production of the original work. Another fine item to appear during the centennial was a solid bronze statue sculpted by Bonita Thien Knickmeyer and released by Liberty Bronze, Inc., of St. Louis. A total of 5000 of these bronzes were earmarked for distribution. Each model, measuring 26 inches high, came serially hand-numbered and sported a hand-rubbed finish. Two models were available, the statuary brown for $595 and the "weathered copper green" for $645, assumedly pre-restoration.

My favorite, however, are the statues marketed throughout 1985 and '86 by an outfit called Mader's Tower Gallery of Milwaukee. The manufacturer had acquired portions of the metal work and cement base that were being trashed during the restoration efforts Mr. Iacocca spoke so eloquently about. And, sure enough, as quickly as you can say "dump it into a mold," a new statue was produced and being offered to the public for $139.50. Officially referred to as an "authentic materials sculpture," each 15-inch statue is "crafted of authentic, irreplaceable metals from Liberty itself," Mader's said, "that until very recently were part of the actual Statue of Liberty in New York Harbor!" Mader's package came complete with the prerequisite "certificate of authenticity" signed by none other than Lee Iacocca himself.

"The" Circus

Lost somewhat in the millions of dollars in fireworks and resounding commotion that accompanied the centenary of the Brooklyn Bridge and Statue of Liberty was the one hundredth anniversary of another American institution, the Ringling Brothers Circus (which ultimately teamed up with the Barnum and Bailey show). An anniversary celebration was staged during the summer of 1983 in Baraboo, Wisconsin, the city often called the "mother of circuses." Today Baraboo houses the Circus World Museum, but a century ago it was the hometown of the five Ringling Brothers—Al, Otto, Alf, Charles, and John—who went on to make circus history. From July 4 to 7, the Ringling Brothers Centennial Association owned Baraboo, drumming up a $65,000 birthday party that included a huge street parade put on in conjunction with the Circus World Museum, as well as fireworks and all the fixin's. The motion picture *The Greatest Show On Earth*, which actually debuted in Baraboo, was shown in town all week. Children of all ages scooped up every sort of memorabilia—which circus collectors will be hotly pursuing for decades hence.

"The" Cola

If you are to believe ads in recent years for Coca-Cola, the soft drink has succeeded in becoming as American as Mom, apple pie, and a Saturday afternoon at the circus all rolled into one. Yet, either through a major miscalculation or a daring desire to accord its new formula a lot of publicity, the folks at Coke opted in 1985 to change the ninety-nine-year-old formula of Coca-Cola, which immediately raised serious questions as to whether the "Real Thing" was in fact the real thing anymore. The "New Coke," which hit supermarket shelves in the spring of 1985, uncapped such a storm of protest that the Atlanta-based company relented and reversed its corporate decision to shelve the original formula. Before the summer was out, old Coke was back, being sold side by side with new Coke, and identified as the original on the label by the addition of the word "Classic." A humorous footnote was a report that a California man drove around local communities buying up caseloads of the soda within hours after the initial news that Coca-Cola was retiring the old taste. His plan was presumably to sell, albeit illegally, bottles and cans containing the "pre-new" Coke to hard-core Coca-Cola fanatics.

When Coke reversed its decision after a few weeks, his market fell apart and he was left with a lot of soda on his hands. To add insult to injury, a survey conducted late in the year showed that "Classic" Coke was outselling the "New Coke" in every portion of the country—except California. I was curious as to whether all this flurry of activity and new labeling could be expected to enhance the value of Coke products produced in 1985. I posed this question to John Buchholz, president of the Cola Clan (5108 Lakespring Dr., Dunwoody, GA 30338), a national collecting society for Coca-Cola collectors, boasting 2500 members. "Not particularly," Buchholz said. "The new labeling really just creates frustration among collectors rather than rare items. Collectors of Coke feel like the hobby has been diluted." What Buchholz and others did feel would be worth adding to Coca-Cola collections in the '80s are commemorative products being sanctioned by Coke as part of its centennial, observed in 1986. Collectors sought advance information on this, but, in Buchholz's words, the company was being "'secretive"—perhaps to avert a great deal of pre-speculation on the part of collectors. The direct marketing outfit, American Family, which does much of its advertising through the pages of the Sunday supplement *Parade* magazine, hit the market with the first of what was to be a small avalanche of items in October 1985: the Coca-Cola Centennial Thermometer. Selling for $9.95, it sported the familiar red-and-white company colors and carried the words "Coca-Cola One Hundredth Anniversary 1886–1986." Coke's franchising of its colors and logo for centennial products was designed to terminate on December 31, 1986. After that point, all centennial memorabilia could be had only through the "secondary market"—i.e., sold secondhand via flea markets and the like. Through this method, the company was able to limit the number and duration of time in which centennial items could be produced, assuring that all items identified as bonafide Coke centennial memorabilia were in fact originally sold during the centennial year.

"The" Singer

America's taste in music during the 1980s was dramatized by the fact that when the New York Metropolitan Opera marked its centennial in October of 1983, the general public hardly blinked. But when the golden anniversary of the birth of Elvis Presley approached, the event heralded the biggest burst of Presley products to emerge since the singing truckdriver from Tupelo first rolled out of the deep south with his guitar over his shoulder and a hint of a sneer on his lips back in the mid 1950s. If Elvis Presley had not died in 1977, the King of Rock 'n' Roll would have marked his

Elvis lives on in collector plates.

fiftieth birthday on January 8, 1985—a fact that hardly passed unnoticed in the general press. Presley's face stared out at us from magazine racks to such a degree that you'd hardly think he was gone.

Rosalind Cranor, of Blacksburg, Virginia, an expert on Elvis Presley and a leading collector of Presleyana, contends that Presley's popularity is as strong today as ever—considering the fact that his appeal now incorporates a wider age group than ever before. After all, the kids who were rocking to "Hound Dog" and "Heartbreak Hotel" back in 1956 are now pushing fifty. The popularity Presley continues to enjoy nearly a decade after his death was perhaps no better pointed out than by *Goldmine* magazine, a record collectors' publication out of Iola, Wisconsin. In January 1985 it ran a list of every Elvis Presley fan club and collecting group it could track down. The list, which included groups like the Blue Hawaiians for Elvis Presley of Los Angeles, Elvis Fans from Hoosierland of Indiana, The Elvis Presley Burning Love Fan Club of Illinois, and the North Jersey Knights for Elvis, numbered over ninety-four active fan clubs around the world.

Elvis gold decanter.

Elvis Gold Encore Decanter made by McCormick.

The fiftieth anniversary of Presley's birth was a potential marketing bonanza. "There were all sorts of items," Mrs. Cranor, author of *Elvis Collectibles,** said. "A lot of the people who are buying the new stuff are fans—people who want to decorate their homes with new Elvis items simply because they like Elvis." Cranor said that these fans have Elvis items "all over their houses." While referring to some of the new memorabilia as "somewhat gaudy" and expressing her own preference for the original '50s memorabilia, she readily admits that more and more of the Presley items being produced today are finding their way into collections.

Fred Whobrey, of Mt. Zion, Illinois, would agree. Whobrey is as close to a lifelong collector of Elvis as you might find. "I started collecting Elvis items when he first came out," Whobrey said. "I was fifteen years old at the time." Today Whobrey continues to add choice new examples of Presleyana to his archives, including items that date back over three decades. Whobrey stays up to date on all the latest Elvis merchandise just as he

*Collector Books, Paducah, Kentucky

Elvis and his horse by the McCormick Distilling Company.

keeps track of the latest going price for an original Presley Emene toy guitar vintage 1957 ($500 to $700) or original Elvis gum cards ($5 to $8 apiece).

Since Elvis became the King of Rock 'n' Roll largely through the medium of records, it seemed appropriate when Whobrey explained that the most desirable Elvis item from the 1980s is a 45 rpm. "Copies of this record were given away to people who toured the Elvis Presley home in Tupelo, Mississippi, back in August of 1982," Whobrey said. On one side of the single is a recording of the King singing "The Im-

possible Dream," while the other side has him singing something called "American Trilogy." "It was the first time that RCA released a record specifically to be a collectible," Whobrey said. "The record sleeve is white and carries only the word 'Elvis' on it and was never commercially released—explaining that it was not for sale on the label." Only 7500 copies were given away, and they can already fetch between $200 and $300. "It's the most desirable Elvis collectible of the '80s."

Another scarce Elvis recording—also a 45 rpm—was released two years later, in August 1984. This record was at first intended to be a mass-released commercial single, but was pulled from distribution by RCA after its debut in Tupelo and Memphis. "It was released as a teaser for their fiftieth-anniversary album," Whobrey said. "It was the first record to carry the 'Elvis 50' logo on it," the collector explained. The two recordings, "Baby, Let's Play House" and "Hound Dog," were in fact live recordings made in September 1956 during an appearance by Presley at the Mississippi-Alabama Dairy Show. On its dust sleeve was a picture of Presley taken during the show. "They pressed 20,000 of the records on gold vinyl and released them only in the two southern cities before they decided to recall them,'' Whobrey said. ''I was in Tupelo when they were released and picked up two, thinking that I'd be able to get more when I got home. Then I heard that they were being recalled.'' The reason for the recall was largely the sound quality of the record, recorded with early live microphones while on location. Whobrey said they ''sound like they would if they had been recorded by a cassette player.'' After considering it, RCA felt that this was not the best release to spin out in advance of the *Elvis Presley: A Golden Celebration* album, slated to be released the following January. ''They sent telegrams to record stores in Tupelo and Memphis telling them to stop sales of the record.'' Whobrey said. Despite RCA's efforts, some 12,000 were distributed and within a year's time were selling for between $25 and $30. By the way, the album that ultimately was released by RCA on Presley's birthday, January 8, 1985, was a remastered version of earlier recordings spread over six LPs. The record package in itself makes no mistake that this release is intended to be something out of

the ordinary, coming as it did in a box with frosted gold gift wrapping with raised gloss swirls forming a portrait of Elvis. As it contained largely unreleased recordings and interviews, it was very popular with Presley fans and experienced brisk sales— despite its $50 retail price upon release.

''Everything RCA did regarding Elvis in 1985 was tied into the golden anniversary,'' Whobrey said. One of the more interesting marketing steps was the company's re-release of the 1957 Presley Christmas album, which pictures gift-wrapped presents. ''From a distance, the new release and the original look identical,'' he explained. ''But

Many Elvis decanters were sold during the 50th anniversary year.

when you look closely at the album's cover you can see that they had to reshoot the cover picture," presumably because the color had faded from the original print and was no longer reproducible. "The ribbons on one of the packages on the new album has a pattern on it that is not on the original package," the collector attested.

Another interesting spinoff of the golden anniversary was produced by an outfit called California Gold Records, who marketed Presley singles and LPs with their original covers under glass, closely resembling gold records. "They were real records sprayed with an actual gold spray," Whobrey said. "They were among the more unique items marketed at the time."

Manufacturers obviously decided that the youngsters who grew up with the King were now solidly in the expendable income bracket and money was no longer of consequence when it came to playtoys. Ads announcing "Elvis ...once again man of the hour," heralded the marketing of limited-edition men's and ladies' watches that were released in honor of the fiftieth by Bradley Time of New York early in 1985. Each watch, featuring a raised-relief picture of Presley singing, microphone

in hand, resembled a coin and came set in an eighteen-karat gold case, priced at $1985 (in honor of the anniversary year). "It's a special tribute to the most outstanding performer and personality of our time," Bradley announced. Further playing on the anniversary date, Bradley promised to provide watches only to "the first 1985 ladies and 1985 men" who decided that "1985 is Elvis Time For Me!"

Perhaps the most unusual, however, and certainly the one that enjoyed the most press coverage at the time, was the $2500 Elvis Presley doll produced by World Doll, Inc. This ultimate in Elvis effigies stands in fact as the crowning product of a series of Elvis dolls produced by this Brooklyn-based company during the fiftieth mania. World Doll, which is a subsidiary of the half-century-old Eugene Doll and Novelty Company, got the idea after their 1983 Marilyn Monroe doll proved to be a considerable success. The Presley doll, which debuted at the New York Toy Fair in February 1984, came in three versions, ranging from the "affordable" $90 model up to the one toting the hefty price tag. A press release issued at the time stated simply that "all will depict the singing idol in his prime''—a no doubt wise marketing move.

The $90 vinyl Elvis came attired in a white suit with gold trim, white boots, and a colored scarf. Accessories included a finger ring, belt buckle, and hand-held microphone. The second model, priced at $225, had porcelain head, hands, and legs, with a "poseable body." This time, Elvis was fitted in a gold lamé suit and gold boots. Each doll was numbered as part of a limited edition. And what did $2500 bring you? Here's Elvis decked out in his best: porcelain from head to toe and dressed in an "Aloha Hawaii" outfit, studded with rhinestones, a diamond in his belt buckle, and a scarf made from an actual one taken from the King's personal wardrobe. But that's not all. Each of the 750 numbered models came packed with an actual ticket from Presley's last concert, June 26, 1977, at Market Square Arena in Indianapolis. Definitely a top-of-the-line collectible.

There's little question that the Elvis market is alive and well in the '80s. An increasing number of companies have discovered that the Presley name is as good as gold. Rosalind Cranor points to the smashing success of the

The $90 vinyl Elvis produced by World Doll.

McCormick Distilling Company of Weston, Missouri, and its ever-expanding line of Elvis whiskey decanters, as an example of this phenomenon in full bloom. "I bought the first few in the series when they

61

came out, but simply couldn't keep up with all of them," Cranor confided. Yet many collectors have, as evidenced by the profusion of variations on the original theme. Billed by McCormick as "the most successful series of decanters every produced," the company has pulled all stops, so to speak, to keep up with the demand. What started as simply a ceramic scale version of the King has grown to include models of Elvis in his karate uniform, in GI wear (complete with a reproduction of Presley's Army dog tags attached to its base), as well as astride his horse Rising Sun. We're talking serious Elvis collectibles here, the zenith of the line being the limited-edition "Fiftieth Birthday Decanter." Standing nearly 18-inches tall, this gold metal statue has Elvis standing atop a wooden base. Encircling the base are gold coins carrying depictions of important people and events in Presley's life. Parents Gladys and Vernon Presley even have their own coin. There's Elvis as a child, one showing Graceland, Elvis in the Army, and so on. The last coin is called "the final chapter, Farewell." This decanter is musically equipped, playing "I Want You, I Need You, I Love You."

How do serious collectors view this rash of Elvis merchandise? With considerable credibility. Fred Whobrey feels that these sorts of items, particularly the limited-edition merchandise, will fare well down the collecting road. "To me, the new things will never replace the old things," he said, "but twenty years from now people will be looking for the new Elvis items. My children collect Elvis—of course they were brought up that way—and I hope that their children will also collect Elvis memorabilia. It's like Michael Jackson. Twenty years from now everyone will be looking for the original memorabilia. And when there are no more to go around, someone will make more. And then someday those will be collectable. These things go in cycles."

5. Music

February 1984. For fans of Michael Jackson, those were happy days. President Ronald Regan, who invited Michael to a White House reception, was in his first term in office. The economy was on the upswing. Millions were still buying Michael's *Thriller* album, which was in its twenty-eighth consecutive week at the top of *Billboard's* LP chart. And Michael's hit single of the same name, featuring a "rap" by horror film veteran Vincent Price, had just become the seventh single spun off the epochal album, which was smashing every record on the books. Michael's monstrous popularity promoted *Time* magazine to break with its long-standing tradition of running a portrait on its cover only when accompanied by an inside interview, and featured Michael on its cover at the hight of Jacksonmania. The magazine had to explain to its readers how it was unsuccessful in attempts to get young Mr. Jackson to speak with them. Alas, his agent told *Time*, Michael was not giving interviews.

Meanwhile, Jackson memorabilia was being unleashed on the young buying crowd through the local Woolworth's and Spencers chain stores, and record stores. Retailers were reporting that summer that Jacksonmania was the biggest thing to hit the rock spinoff trade since the Beatles. Just as yesterday's Beatles wigs and "I Love Ringo" buttons once took the nation by storm, it seemed for a while that Michael was everywhere—white sequined gloves, dolls, *Thriller* buttons, and the like abounded.

That year Laurel Wang was just one of millions of Michael fans collecting Jacksoniana. Wang was president of Michael's official fan organization, Jackson's World Club, which kept the superstar's fans in touch with the aid of a newsletter. It also made available to them posters, buttons, and T-shirts—all with the approval of Mr. Jackson' official licensing coordinator. Entertainer's Merchandise Management Corporation (EMMC). Wang was quoted that year as saying that her fan club was one of a handful of outlets to receive clearance to sell Jackson merchandise. All official merchandise carried on it

"EMMC," "MMJ Productions," or "Triumph Merchandise." Any others were impostors, Wang explained, and at first there were many. In May 1984, *USA Today* reported that Michael had finally begun cracking down. "Since May 11," the newspaper noted, "agents for Jackson have confiscated more than $5 million worth of phony posters, sunglasses, and clothing from warehouses, department stores, and flea markets in New York. But there is at least $50 million worth of fake Jackson goods across the USA, officials say." The newspaper quoted Jackson's New York lawyer, Stephen Huff, who said his client "is concerned that the public doesn't get cheap, inferior goods."

So what about those quality items one could legally acquire? Among the profusion of goods, one product stands out: the Michael Jackson doll released during the summer of 1984, produced by LJN Toys of New York. Company spokesperson Liz Wardley was quoted earlier that year as saying that LJN had already received advance orders for "several million dolls" and it was anticipated "a few million more" orders would come in before the doll actually hit store shelves. The box con-

taining Michael in his Grammy Awards outfit explained that the doll was "fully poseable," allowing the owner to "recreate his famous dance step"—the very same moon-

Michael Jackson doll, featuring his Grammy Awards outfit.

walk he thrilled a nation with during the Motown Special in 1983. The doll retailed for $14 and LJN also marketed three additional outfits, described as the "Thriller," "Beat It" and "Billie Jean" attire. For possible comparison, it might be pointed out that Beatle dolls produced in 1964 by the Remko company (originally selling for $2 to $3 apiece) were showing up at collectibles shows in the mid-'80s for as much as $850 per doll.

Rock Hits the Big-time Auctions

Even as teenagers crowded jewelry counters in shopping malls around the nation, buying up white-sequined Michael gloves by the fistful, rock memorabilia was making dramatic inroads in some most unexpected places—not the least of which was the venerable auction gallery Sotheby's. Through both its New York and London galleries, Sotheby's has succeeded in bringing to auction assorted rock music memorabilia, thereby thrusting such items into an entirely new realm of legitimacy. It began in 1981 when the London gallery reported selling John Lennon's piano for $15,200 and reached new heights in June 1985 when a Canadian businessman pur-

chased the Beatles' psychedelic limo at Sotheby's New York gallery for the incredible sum of $2.29 million. I had the good fortune of being present at a number of the collectibles auctions at Sotheby's New York gallery, including the one when the first rock memorabilia passed over their block. At first, Sotheby's displayed some caution in the amount of rock items it handled, often assuring a crowd would be on hand by sandwiching them between more time-tested collectibles, like dolls. I remember just such a sale at Sotheby's in June 1982. The first session consisted largely of dolls, with a considerable contingent of Brus and Jumeaus attracting brisk bidding. Then it came time for Beatles memorabilia to be sold. Copies of the Beatles' *Butcher* album, showing the Fab Four holding dismembered dolls and raw meat, were among the lots. I witnessed that day what surely must have been the most dramatic changing of the guards in auction history. In a matter of moments, large clusters of blue-haired women abruptly left their seats, replaced by a motley crew of Beatle buffs, some clad for the occasion in leather jackets and boots. It had taken twenty years for

Beatles fans to get this far.

Unlike the Beatles, it did not take the passage of two decades for Michael Jackson to make his debut within the auspicious setting of a leading auction house. The honor of being the first major gallery to bring Jacksoniana to bids belongs to the Charles Hamilton Galleries of New York. Hamilton, who specializes in autographs, earned this distinction when he listed a "White Glove Autographed by Michael Jackson" among the 192 lots he brought before the public at an auction held on November 29, 1984. It seems that this was not one of the sequined variety. In fact, the glove apparently originally belonged to an elevator operator. It was signed by Jackson in blue ink (he drew a star next to his signature) and also by his brother, Jermaine, after being presented to Michael by his personal elevator operator at a New York hotel where the Jacksons were staying. Hamilton's catalog placed a presale estimate of between $250 and $300 on the right-handed glove, saying that "the fingers of the glove are soiled [but the glove is] otherwise in fine condition." The glove sold for $525.

The following spring, Jackson memorabilia was again making the New York auction scene, this time when a promotional award for his *Thriller* album, consisting of a platinum album surrounded by three gold 45 rpms and a letter written by Michael, sold for $2200 at Sotheby's. The letter, which was addressed to someone identified as "Tom," read: "We are all part of history in the making. *Thriller* is one of the biggest albums ever. Thank you for your support, effort and hard work." The missive was signed by the superstar and encased in a plexiglass frame with a photo of Jackson.

The most recent piece of Jacksonabilia I saw surface came from an unexpected quarter. Somewhat quietly, a philatelic periodical filed a report in July 1985 that the British Virgin Islands was issuing a set of eight postage stamps that month featuring American pop star Michael Jackson. (Had they just received their shipment of Michael dolls?) The report mentioned the noteworthy value of the stamp, marking as it did the first time that the Queen's head had not appeared on a British Virgin Islands stamp. Other than this and an appearance during the taping of the video for "We Are the World" (which he co-wrote), Michael

Jackson dropped out of the news altogether during 1985. *Rolling Stone* magazine, in its year-end issue, ran a story that asked, "Whatever happened to Michael Jackson?" "The year 1985 has been a black hole for Michael watchers, who witnessed the most spectacular disappearing act since Halley's comet headed for the far side of the solar system in 1910," the magazine reported. It further observed that "remainder tables still groan beneath unsold Michael calendars, and a Fifth Avenue toy store was palming off clothes for the Michael Jackson doll as disco outfits for Ken." I decided to contact Jackson's World Club to find out what was happening. My letter went unanswered. A call to Epic Records, Michael's label, indicated that "the Jackson fan club has temporarily disbanded"; it hoped to get back together sometime in '86, in time for the release of Michael's third solo album.

The Lesser Lights

In the ephemeral world of rock music, today's superstar is often tomorrow's washed-up act. While no one else, so far in the decade, has reached the heights attained by Jackson during his peak, certainly Prince, Madonna, and Bruce Springsteen have come close and, to lesser degrees, Boy George and Cyndi Lauper have enjoyed their moments in the sun.

Madonna earned her place as the mid-'80s most popular female performer and, in so doing, won a place in the heart of Biz Reed. Reed is a Lynnfield, Massachusetts, music collector who has spent the past couple of years actively searching for anything and everything related to the career of Madonna. Reed began collecting Madonna mementoes during the summer of 1984, just as her hit single "Borderline" began climbing the charts. "What I've accumulated so far are promotional things—buttons, posters (as large as 10 feet by 3 feet), display items from record stores, bin dividers, a lot of paper type of goods." A good number of the items Reed has tracked down have come as a result of advertising in national record collecting periodicals. "I hear from Madonna collectors all over the country." A collector on the West Coast sent Reed a quartz desk clock that sports a picture of Madonna in concert on its face.

Like many music collectors, Reed is attempting to collect sounds as well as objects. "I'm trying to locate some early audio when she was with a couple of bands in New York before she really hit it big. She was with a group called Breakfast. They did a little work for a while and I'm trying to track down possible recordings which were made then." He explained that if such recordings are to be found, they'd be on tapes, not records. Of the post-fame period, Reed said, "She hit it so big so quickly after that first record that they pressed all of her records in vast numbers and the records themselves are everywhere." He does advise collectors to hold on to the original illustrated paper sleeves from Madonna's single releases, which traditionally appreciate in value more quickly than the records they are designed to protect.

Due to the sheer number of records sold in this country, collectors like Biz Reed have had to search import record bins and other sources to find unusual recordings. Reed's searching has turned up promo records containing a mix of interviews and music. "These were produced for airplay on the radio and not released to the public," he explained. His prized possession, however, is a 1983 gold album award that honored the

singer's first album, titled simply *Madonna*. "These are presented to industry employees on a very limited basis."

Of the roughly one hundred items Reed had in his collection when I spoke with him, two were not included: the copies of *Playboy* and *Penthouse* released in 1985 containing nude photos of Madonna. "I wasn't interested in that type of thing," he said. "Of the other collectors I've talked to, they all said that they really didn't pay much attention to them as they were more of a sensational thing."

The staying power of stars like Michael Jackson or Madonna is often based on what publicists call the "visibility factor." While agents work overtime to gain valuable publicity for their clients, publicity often happens quite by chance. Take the case of the Beach Boys early in the decade. As everyone knows, the Beach Boys first made music waves back in the '60s with a string of hits that included "Surfin' USA," "I Get Around," and "California Girls." In the years since, the group has managed to remain together in nearly its original form, despite the death of drummer Dennis Wilson early this decade. In 1983, the Beach Boys burst back into the limelight thanks to a national flap caused by then Secretary of the Interior James Watt. It all began when Mr. Watt decided to ban the boys from appearing at the annual July Fourth celebration held on the grounds of the Washington Monument, claiming that the group would attract "undesirable elements." First Lady Nancy Reagan came to the Beach Boys' rescue, saying that she liked their music. In the end, the Beach Boys were welcomed back to Washington and Mr. Watt exited his post—only to surface again in a small news story late in 1984. It seems that Mr. Watt autographed a Beach Boys album at a Reagan-Bush rally. The album was eventually auctioned off for $105 to raise money for the Sheridan, Wyoming, County Library, and purchased by one Larry Mehlhaff, a Sierra Club representative. "This album will be a true collector's item," Mehlhaff was quoted as saying.

The New World of MTV and Other Visual Aids to Music

The most important news in the music field during the decade did not come across the auction block. It came across our television screen, centering around the widespread ac-

ceptance and resulting impact embodied in three letters: MTV. MTV, short for Music Television, is indisputably the most important development in popular music since the advent of the 45 rpm record. Its force during the '80s has turned music into a visual medium: it is now more important than ever for rock stars to look like movie stars. If they can act like movie stars too, well, look out. Here is where Michael Jackson's legacy may in fact remain. His dynamic video for the hit single "Beat It" turned the infant video medium around. No longer was it acceptable for rock stars to simply mug into the camera as they mouthed the words of their songs, à la Mick Jagger. Their movements were now choreographed, and story lines were developed to match the words of their songs. Performers were being showcased as never before. In the end, even Jagger threw in the towel and took entire film crews to exotic South American locales to film videos for the latest Rolling Stones releases.

As early as 1981, the music industry was attempting to gauge the inevitable impact videos would have on the record business in general. Some were predicting that year that the phonograph record as we know it will be obsolete by the year 1990, replaced by compact videocassettes that "show" your favorite hits. While there still seems to be a good deal of vinyl in the music stores at this juncture of the decade, there is no question that the record industry has been in a tailspin for many years. If video does render a death blow to records, it will only come after years of the competitive pounding records have been receiving from the tape field. Stop by your local record store sometime soon and you'll be surprised at the diminished role records play. It is presently very difficult to find 45 rpm records in most music stores, while LPs seem to be losing ground more and more to cassette tapes. One record industry spokesman was quoted as lamenting, "What we may be witnessing is the end of an era begun with Thomas Edison."

During the early '80s, beleaguered record officials were forced to explore new ways to convince the basically young music buyers who support the billion-dollar industry to bring back their traditional market. The decade has seen considerable experimentation with the color, sizes, and shapes of records. In 1981, the group Po-lice released singles from their album *Zenyatta Mondatta* in the shape of a badge. Only a few thousand were produced and became hot items in record stores. Of these fads, the revival of the picture disc was perhaps accorded the greatest acceptance. For a while, everything from the music of John Williams of the Boston Pops to rereleases of Beatles albums were turning up as picture discs.

The concept of picture discs has been around for a long time, with the earliest examples actually first emerging in Nazi Germany in the 1930s. In the late 1940s, 78-rpm picture discs became something of a sensation in this country largely through the release of the Vogue picture records, sold through Macy's and the like. Picture discs began reappearing in the late 1970s. It was during this time that Pic Disc, a leading producer of these colorful musical incarnations, came into existence, manufacturing its first products in 1977. The process of creating picture discs, as employed by Pic Disc and others, is simple enough, involving the lamination of printed paper inside sound-reproducing material. It is a slow process, which is done by hand on a compression-molding machine. Items produced by Pic Disc ranged from a scented strawberry-shaped record by Rufus to a sixteen-year-old speech by Ronald Reagan, with a laminated picture of the President.

During the height of the picture disc revival, Pic Disc received permission to go back into the vaults and produce picture-disc versions of some of rock music's classics. At that time, the company issued a souvenir edition of the Beatles' *Sergeant Pepper's Lonely Hearts Club Band* album in a 150,000 pressing. The record retailed for $16, but demand for the novelty among Beatles collectors was such that one New York record store intentionally jacked up the retail price of the record—and flaunted the fact. A sign posted near the display read, "List price, $15.98. Our price, $24.95...while they last." They were quickly sold out.

Wayne Johnson of Rockaway Records in Los Angeles said it didn't take long for some of the latest round of picture discs to appreciate in value. The most valuable of these, by today's market standards, actually predates the '80s by a couple of years. One is a ten-inch special promotional sound track recording from the Gene Kelly and Olivia

Newton-John movie, *Xanadu*. The record, which featured a picture of Olivia Newton-John, was produced by Pic Disc in a quantity of fifty (as compared to the normal minimum pressing of 1000). "When they were new, I was selling them for about $150," Johnson said. "Now I'm selling them for about $450." Perhaps the most valuable to come out of this era is a Paul McCartney picture disc. "It is super rare and as it was released by a former Beatle, it is in great demand by Beatles collectors,"

E.T. Picture Disc: music to look for extraterrestrials by.

Johnson explained. The record was released in a limited edition of 100 and was issued at the same time as the McCartney album *Back To The Egg*. Most people who have managed to get a hold of one have refused to part with it. "I'm one of the few persons who ever sold one," Johnson said. How much did it fetch? "I'll just say that it was over $1000," he said.

Odd-shaped records and picture discs continued to find a market as the industry moved into the second half of the decade. "The American picture disc market just is not like it used to be," Johnson said. "I'd say that 90 percent of the picture discs now coming out are made in other countries—the United Kingdom, Germany, places where they remain very popular." American record buyers have become more discriminating about novelties. "Today a picture disc is going to sell well only if it is an unusual record by a McCartney or Springsteen, whereas five years ago people would buy a really unusually shaped record by someone they may never have heard of, simply because it was unique." After all, as Johnson surmised, with some 5000 variations of these records already produced, "it is

Picture discs made by Pic Disc.

no longer a novelty, is it? It seems every shape imaginable has been done." This is brought out by a quick inventory check of some of the discs Rockaway had on hand when I spoke with them, including a square-shaped record of Billy Idol's *Rebel Yell*, the Rolling Stones' *She Was Hot* (tongue-shaped), and Elton John's *Sad Songs* (hat-shaped)—all British-made and fetching $6 apiece. The earlier Police record of "Message In a Bottle" (in the shape of a six-pointed badge) was now fetching $20. Most 7-inch picture discs were selling for under $10, while 12-

inch picture discs averaged $10, including the sound track record from *Footloose*, Jackson's *Thriller* album and Culture Club's *Colour By Numbers*.

Of all the novelties rushed onto the market during the late '70s and early '80s, one stands out as Wayne Johnson's favorite: a special issue of the Police's *Ghost in the Machine* (1981). The regular LP featured three red digital symbols on a black field. But the special pressings featured a built-in lighting effect, as explained by Johnson: "When you put the record on the turntable, little red lights lit up and flashed, forming the same symbols as on the album cover. The switch was in the hole in the center of the record, so it was activated when you put the metal turntable spindle through it."

Music And Social Themes

Music and social woes, a dominant theme of the pop music scene in the '60s, was almost entirely forgotten during the '70s when the "Me Generation" raced off to be outfitted for disco suits and learned to emulate the gyrations we saw in *Saturday Night Fever*. Social issues returned to the pop music world during the mid-'80s when record sales were pushed to help a myriad of ills in the global community, including famine in Africa, the plight of the American farmer, and South African apartheid. Marketing was a big part of the various efforts, as money from the sales of everything from "We Are the World" sweatshirts to printed programs from Live Aid were funneled into the cause.

The '80s social record phenomenon actually got its first strong foothold in England, when a group of rock stars got together to record "Do They Know It's Christmas?" under the name BandAid. Sales for the record went to African famine relief efforts. Early in 1985, American recording artists assembled in a recording studio after the Grammy Awards telecast and recorded "We Are the World." Both efforts came together on July 13, 1985, when sixty-one of rock's biggest acts performed in two large outdoor stadiums, in Philadelphia and London. The event was beamed live to an estimated worldwide radio and television audience of 1.5 billion people. The Live Aid concert reportedly raised about $55 million dollars. Meanwhile, 88,000 country music fans came together in

Champaign, Illinois, that September for FarmAid, a musical fundraiser for the American farmer. By year's end, on a record called "Sun City," Bob Dylan, Keith Richards, Ringo Starr, Bruce Springsteen, and fifty other acts were singing out against apartheid.

The consensus of record collectors is that the recordings themselves, such as "We Are the World" (which remained on the top of *Billboard's* charts for a month) sold so many copies that they in themselves will not hold out much value. On the other hand, merchandise from the records, including clothing, posters, and other paraphernalia, will fare better than most items from the music field simply because of the impact the recording had on the decade. Speaking of the Live Aid concert, one record collector said, "It was the biggest thing since Woodstock." By the way, posters from the Woodstock Music and Art Fair and movie, released a year afterward, average $150 to $200 apiece when they surface at auction in New York today. Of course, Woodstock didn't have a fraction of the marketing muscle thrown into gear for Live Aid. Yet it is a safe bet that memorabilia from the '80's answer to Yasgur's farm will be turning up

at leading galleries in the near future—very likely before the end of the decade. The sort of items likely to command the greatest interest are signed programs and other promotional material actually dated from the events. Autograph hounds were in high gear both at Wembley Stadium in London and the John F. Kennedy Stadium in Philadelphia during Live Aid and the fruits of their toils will no doubt be turning up for years.

Tips About Music Collectibles

The nice thing about rock music in general and record collecting in particular is that they both have been around a long time. And as is the case with anything that has passed through a couple of generations of collectors, certain reoccurring guidelines are established—trends that hold true whether you are talking about the days of Ivory Joe Hunter, Manfred Mann, or Duran Duran. With over 2000 records in my collection, I've found myself relying on a check list of buzz words whenever I find myself flipping at lightning speed through stacks of secondhand records in some dusty corner of a junkshop. One word about junkshops: be prepared to wade through a lot of junk. I swear I've seen more Shaun and David Cassidy records in my day than anyone else short of Shirley Jones. And remember Bobby Sherman? Nobody wants his stuff, either. Same holds true with the Babys, the Bay City Rollers, and somebody called Leif Garrett. Moral: don't collect pre-teen schlock. These records die of loneliness in cutout record bins all around the country.

On the other hand, when flipping through records, look for words which read "Not For Sale," "Disk Jockey Copy," "Promotional Record," or some comparable variation. If it's *Sasame Yuki* by Hiroshi Itsuki or *Orizzonti Perduti* by Franco Battiato, go on to the next record. But if it's *Say, Say, Say* by Paul McCartney and Michael Jackson, or a pre-release album of *She's So Unusual* by Cyndi Lauper, set it aside. Promotional records for any song that eventually broke the top ten are a good bet.

If you feel you've kept yourself fairly up to date on popular music, yet you happen upon the 45 rpm of a song you've never heard of by an otherwise popular group or recording artist, purchase it if you feel the price is right. Chances are either it is (a) an early effort by a star or group recorded before fame and fortune struck; (b) a flop single issued between hits, such as Bruce Springsteen's "Fade Away"—which did just that after it hit the 20 position on *Billboard* in 1981; or (c) a trial record that never saw actual commercial release. Of these, the last would prove to be the most desirable, from a collecting standpoint.

Picture sleeves for 45 rpms are another record collectible with a good case history behind it. Any Elvis or Beatles collector worth his salt would mortgage his home for a chance to own complete runs of all the picture sleeves issued with the original singles. If you still have original sleeves for 45s by Jackson, Lauper, Madonna, et al., take them out of your record box right away and put them in a safe place. Also in the paper field are album stuffers, including posters and decals, which often come packaged in an album as a bonus. Chances are you'll find a million *Purple Rain* albums by Prince and the Revolution, but try to find the original poster that came with it.

Twelve-inch singles, which got their birth during the disco era, have a good chance of becoming collectable. Most contemporary singles are being issued for two different markets, the Top 40 crowd and the dance audience. The traditional 45 rpm continues to service the former, while the longer remix versions show up in leading record shops in the larger 12-inch single, which might be made for play at 33 1/3 speed or 45 rpms. A typical 12-inch single actually can offer three or more versions of the same song, such as the 1984 12-incher of *Dancing in the Dark* by Bruce Springsteen, which includes "Radio," "Dub," and "Blaster Mix" versions. The people who run record stores say that these dance-oriented versions of popular hits don't sell as well as 45s, LPs, and tapes, consequently they will be more difficult to acquire in the years ahead.

One more area to consider is movie sound tracks. Among the most desirable albums from the 1950s, after Elvis Presley's, are those from motion pictures. Time seems to place a double dose of nostalgia on these recordings, which are popular with both record connoisseurs and film buffs. The '80s has seen phenomenal success accorded film sound track albums, including those from *Flashdance*, *Footloose*, and *Beverly Hills Cop*— all of which had numerous hit singles spinoffs. They were so successful, in fact, that it will be decades before we can expect to see any premium attached to their value, simply because so many were made. Look instead to the sound tracks issued, without much notice, to accompany the release of a popular film, such as the sound track album to *Raiders of the Lost Ark*. And while we are on the subject of Indiana Jones...

6. Hollywood and the Tube

Star Wars and Star Trek

I first met Indiana Jones at a comic book and science fiction convention in Boston late in 1981. As I recall, Spiderman, Superman, and Darth Vader were also there, but it was Indy who was grabbing the greatest attention. Television stations who sent crews to cover the annual show were lining up to have a word with Mr. Jones, who agreed to provide film crews with the obligatory crack of his whip upon demand. That evening on the Boston newscasts, you hardly knew that Spiderman and his cohorts were at the show, with Mr. Jones getting all the airtime.

I still marvel at the cleverness of the kid (he looked about seventeen or eighteen years old) who opted to come to the show that year dressed as Indiana Jones, but it turned out to be his passport to fleeting fame on Boston television. That had been the year of *Raiders of the Lost Ark* and Indiana Jones was everywhere. Vendors at the show were selling everything from posters and stills from the film to dolls and articles of apparel, and kids and young adults

Raiders of the Lost Ark movie magazine.

were buying up the stuff by the armfuls. An outfit called P & S Sales out of Chapel Hill, North Carolina, perhaps scored the biggest marketing coup when it received rights from Lucasfilms Ltd. to market the "Indiana Jones Authentic Hat," which was in fact your basic Stetson. "Indiana Jones risked his arm for this fedora," the company's advertisements in magazines read, "but you can get it with ease, for just $24.95!" Another brisk-selling piece of *Raiders* merchandise was the Indiana Jones action figure. Priced to sell at $19.95, this 11 1/2-inch doll came complete with removable felt hat, shirt, "leather-look jacket," gun, whip, holster, pants, and boots. "Take your Indiana Jones action figure down into the Well of Souls, or through the insidious booby traps of the ancient Mayan Temple!" the imaginative ad copy for the Indy doll suggested; Well of Souls and Mayan Temple not included.

The crest of popularity accorded Indy and Luke Skywalker, or even Yoda, the Gremlins, or the Ewoks for that matter, traces its origin to the late '60s. The film was

Planet of the Apes, and with its popularity came the realization that there was big money to be made by targeting major motion pictures toward the under-30 age group. A good gauge of the impact of any film on the youth of a nation is the abundance of movie-related costumes worn by youngsters during the first Halloween following a film's release. The sequels—*Return to the Planet of the Apes*, *Beneath the Planet of the Apes*, and so on—assured the costume industry it had a winner in the junior simian suits. Nothing came close until the release of *Star Wars* in 1977. The subsequent releases of *The Empire Strikes Back* and *Return of the Jedi* have kept the demand for Skywalker, C-3PO, R2D2, and the ever popular Vader costumes steady during the Halloween costume marketing through most of the past decade.

With such a multitude of *Star Wars* items marketed through the '80s—everything from Yoda hand puppets and miniature replicas of the deadly attack walkers to a series of *Empire* party plates sold for $1.50—it is difficult to anticipate which ones will ultimately win the favor of future collectors. But in at least one celebrated incident, advance memorabilia from the third film in the series experienced immediate stratospheric prices. A collecting frenzy was touched off in February 1983, when Lucasfilms Ltd. announced that it was changing the name of its then-about-to-be-released sequel in which

E.T. *pinback.*

the cuddly Ewoks would be introduced. Up until that point, it had been referred to as *Revenge of the Jedi*. Press releases announced that henceforth it would be known as *Return of the Jedi*.

Throughout 1982, prerelease promotional materials bearing the approval of Lucasfilms floated out onto the market, all carrying the *Revenge* title. Among these were some 8800 advance posters for the film. A total of 2000 were distributed to motion picture theaters for display in their

Empire Strikes Back party plates.

lobbies during Christmas '82. Another 6800 went to the official Star Wars Fan Club. A spokesman for the club, who was quoted at the time gasping "I've never seen anything like it," reported that his club was offering to its members one-sheet *Revenge* posters just before the title was changed for $9.50. When the news hit, the demand became so intense that its allocation of 6800 was quickly sold out and prices began soaring on the secondary market. Prices of over $100 were commonplace, with a few said to have been priced for as much as $400. Fueling the demand were rumors circulating among *Star Wars* collectors that Lucasfilms had secured a portion of returned posters sent back to the National Screen Service

Yoda hand puppet made by Kenner.

after their display and shredded them.

According to science fiction dealer Jeff Maynard, in the battle for the conquest of outer space memorabilia, a duel between "Star Trek" and *Star Wars* will see Captain Kirk and the crew of the U.S.S. *Enterprise* victorious every time. Maynard runs a leading memorabilia dealership, New Eye Studio of Willimantic, Connecticut, dealing exclusively in what he identifies as "media science fiction." " 'Star Trek' is far and away the king," he said. "There is no comparison between it and *Star Wars*." Maynard said overall the *Star Wars* secondary market has remained pretty flat during off periods between films. Among the few hot items, he said, are ceramic merchandise. These include a set of twelve figurines from *Return of the Jedi*, which sold originally for $10 each, and mug set, also issued in a set of twelve for $8.50 each. "Also popular are the *Star Wars* dolls," Maynard went on to say. "The IG88 (robot) doll from this series can pull close to $300, while all the other *Star Wars* dolls can bring in close to $100; the small ones now bring in about $20." In *Star Wars* merchandise, these are the exceptions.

E.T. *party napkins.*

On the other hand, Maynard said, very few "Star Trek" items fail to command collector prices these days. "About the only thing from 'Star Trek' that dealers find impossible to sell are coloring books and children's clothes—like socks. They just don't seem to appreciate in value." Everything else, however, is "pure gold," reported Maynard. His feeling that "Star Trek" will outprice *Star Wars* stems basically from the sheer longevity of the "Star Trek" phenomenon, which originated when the show first went on the air in 1966 and gained new impetus as a result of the publicity stemming from the three motion pictures released in the '80s reuniting the original cast. He also doesn't dismiss the power of reruns. "We find new fans coming in constantly," he said. "The new films have had a terrific impact in bringing new collectors into this field. And the new generation of kids are also watching the old reruns on television every day. That's the problem with *Star Wars*— it hasn't been a constant series, and it doesn't have television backup between films."

The first merchandise marketed for "Star Trek" dates back to 1969. "Most of the products came out after

1976," Maynard said, stepping up substantially after *Star Wars* broke into the toy market. "Science fiction films used to be viewed as a lost market," he explained. "In the '50s they hardly did anything. It was only in the '70s and '80s that merchandising really started to come into science fiction." At first, things did not look rosy for the revived "Star Trek" films. The first of the new films, *Star Trek—The Motion Picture*, left a bad taste in the mouth of confirmed Trekkies. The story line seemed bent on bringing in the original cast from the TV

The '80s hottest selling Star Trek *items are collector plates.*

show early on and having them systematically replaced by a new crew of fresh-faced younger actors. "It was a really bad movie," Maynard said. A major producer of "Star Trek" items at the time was Mego. "Mego produced a really beautiful set of 'Star Trek' dolls and when the first film flopped so badly, Mego ended up remaindering them. They had to have lost an awful lot of money on those dolls." Not long after, the company went out of business. "That first film nearly killed the market," Maynard went on to say. But that's not to say that the products produced as a result of the first film aren't worth something. "We now get $50 or $60 for those dolls that they remaindered at $2 apiece," he said, explaining that there are six 12-inch dolls in the set, Kirk, Spock, Ilia, Decker, a Klingon, and an alien.

There have been very few items produced in connection with the second and third films, *The Wrath of Khan* (1982) and *The Search for Spock* (1984). "The Ertl company is producing very cheap little 3-inch dolls," Maynard told us, "but there is not much else being manufactured. I think that companies felt so burned on that first film that no one other than Ertl has got-

Star Trek *collector plate issued by Ernst Enterprises.*

ten behind marketing." He did say that the fans continue to produce items, including "fanzines" (containing chatty columns about the old episodes and new motion pictures), which they trade among themselves. "There's only 400 or 500 of these items produced at a time and they are very popular and very collectable."

Current companies have even gone back to the old television shows to come up with new "Star Trek" products. This point was made by "Star Trek" collector Eric Stillwell of Beverly Hills, California. Stillwell favors "Star Trek" music and says that for years it was harder to find than chicken's teeth, as so little was produced. In 1985, record companies began releasing original music taken right off the original '60s episodes. "I believe that these records will become classic 'Star Trek' collectibles from the '80s," he said. These include the original sound track from the pilots "The Cage" and "Where No Man Has Gone Before," released by GNP Record Co., Inc., of Los Angeles. Two other companies that appeared in '85 were Varese Sarabande Records, Inc., of North Hollywood, with sound track scores newly recorded by the Royal Philharmonic Orchestra, and symphonic suites arranged from the original TV scores and pressed by Fifth Continent Music Corp., of Walnut Creek, California.

Perhaps the most popular "Star Trek" merchandise of all time, however, comes from a field that has up until the '80s remained as distant from the science fiction world as Andromeda is to South Bend. Yet the candidate for the bestselling "Star Trek" items of all time are in fact limited edition plates, a form of collectibles that until recently were associated with retirees with china cabinets. "The 'Star Trek' plates have been an absolutely blown-away, unqualified success," said Maynard. "Everyone's collecting the series. It's been one of the best items we've ever carried." The series, painted by Susie Morton, is the brainchild of Ernst Enterprises, a California-based producer of limited-edition plates and figurines. The series debuted in 1984 with the Mr. Spock plate, showing a striking portrait of the famed Vulcan, while the border design of the plate carried the motto of the Starship *Enterprise*: "To boldly go where no man has gone before." The second showed McCoy, the third featured Sulu, and on through the cast, ending the eight plate series with a group portrayal of the cast and the *Enterprise*. As they came on the market, Maynard and other dealers were selling them for $29.50. "They are now going to start a new series showing scenes from 'Star Trek,' " Maynard explained. "That means that the old series will come to an end, and then the prices should double overnight—that's my guess." Maynard feels that the plate represents a good investment for the future, as do sound track albums from the films, copies of the annual "Star Trek" calendar, and anything being made of ceramics or metal ("such as the 'Star Trek'

medallion"). " 'Star Trek' is going to be around a long time," he opined. As he pointed out, the box-office success accorded the two films which followed the near-fatal *Star Trek—The Motion Picture* has assured a fourth film will be made. For Paramount, its gamble to revive the "Star Trek" formula in the '80s is paying off.

Back to the Silents

Perhaps an even greater gamble taken in the age of *Star Wars* and the *Rocky* epochs is the revival of a formula as old as the motion picture itself: silent films. This decade witnessed ambitious efforts to bring before modern audiences two of the greatest silent films ever made, Abel Gance's *Napoleon* and the great-granddaddy of all science fiction films, *Metropolis* (1926). While not the commercial successes of a Luke Skywalker or Rocky Balboa, these two chestnuts from the film vault produced some fine examples of cinemabilia. And for *Metropolis*, it also created some huzzahs the moment it was announced that the "restored" version featured a sound track consisting solely of rock music. Movie buffs cringed at the mere thought of Composer Giorgio Moroder (who wrote the music for *Flashdance*) tampering with the science fiction epic by adding the contemporary sound track. Consequently, it was a curious group of film scholars, old film buffs, and orange-haired rockers who stood in the ticket line during the film's premiere at New York's 57th Street Playhouse in 1984. Inside, the credits for the silent film filled the darkened screen, followed by the music of Adam Ant, Pat Benatar, and Loverboy booming from speakers in Dolby Stereo.

Metropolis *re-release movie poster.*

Fritz Lang's film vision of the future turned out to be one of the surprise hits of the late summer movie season in assorted cities where it played. Moroder readily admitted he got the idea for the revamped *Metropolis* after the success of Francis Ford Coppola's rerelease of the 1927 French masterpiece *Napoleon*, which toured major cities in 1981. The film, which ran over four hours, included new music composed and performed live by Carmine Coppola and a full orchestra. During the showings, finely produced posters were sold and programs distributed—collectibles that have already begun spiraling in value. The *Metropolis* poster, printed by Continental Lithograph of Cleveland, features a Nikosey interpretation of the metallic woman created during the film, done in stunning gold on a blue background. The souvenir *Napoleon* poster was the product of Zoetrope Studios and features an oil painting by Alex Tavoularis depicting actor Albert Dieudonné in the title role. Due to the limited engagements of both films, posters are already difficult to come by and a favorite with classic film collectors and the print crowd, capable of fetching between $40 and $50 by

Napoleon *movie poster from 1981.*

mid-decade—four to five times their original sale price.

An Orphan—Again

Not all revivals fared as well. One of the biggest box office disasters of the decade was set in motion when Columbia decided to bring Harold Gray's little girl with the zero eyes to the silver screen. The move to film *Annie* was preceded by the famous orphan's successful run on Broadway during the late '70s. Get the right kid and a cute dog and you can't miss, director John Huston reasoned. For more than a year before its re-lease, every facet of the production of *Annie* was hyped, beginning with the selection of ten-year-old Aileen Quinn from a gaggle of young aspirants to play the starring role. All during this time, Rastar Films, Inc., was lining up contract after contract to make sure the new *Annie* would be highly visible. "We expect to rival *Star Wars* with the volume of promotional items produced," reported a spokesman for Rastar at the time. Hi-C Fruit Drinks would offer a wall poster of Annie and Sandy for six proof-of-purchase seals. Ovaltine, sponsors of Annie during her radio days, was releasing new Orphan Annie shake-up cups

Annie movie magazine.

85

that would tie into the film's release. The American Library Association soon was issuing hundreds of thousands of bookmarks, featuring Miss Quinn in costume below the word "Read," to children's departments of libraries all over the country. Red wigs were rushed into production by the Knickerbocker Toy Company of New Jersey, retailing for just under $6 in a box that assured "One size fits all." *Annie* dolls hit toy counters bearing $11.50 price tags. By Christmas 1980, *Annie* products were everywhere. Then, in May 1981, the bottom dropped out. The $25-million film premiered at a hundred theaters around the country and was roundly panned. Licensee commitments were such that word quickly surfaced that a new *Annie* film would be produced to bolster sales of the tons of products

Annie wig for kids.

collecting dust on store shelves. Finally, in 1985, it was announced that Miss Quinn had long since grown out of the role and, alas, there would be no new *Annie* after all.

And what of all that *Annie* memorabilia? Being based on a character that has been a part of American pop culture for some fifty-five years, the more interesting products can be expected to fetch respectable prices when they turn up at collector shows in the future. "Annie is a popular character," one New York collectibles shop owner told me. "I suspect you'll see the stuff from the movie attract interest in the years ahead. After all, even though a lot of things were produced, an awful lot of it never sold. So there is not as much around today as you might think."

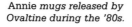

Annie mugs released by Ovaltine during the '80s.

The Lone Ranger— Again

Box office bombs represent a challenging field for the collector. During the summer of 1981, for example, Universal endeavored to revive the Masked Rider of the Plains amid much ballyhoo when it released *The Legend of the Lone Ranger*. The anticipated release of the film brought to the market a flood of Lone Ranger toys and games. It quickly became clear, however, that the film was as stale as two-day-old popcorn. Wholesalers pulled the new Lone Ranger products from their shelves. Wise was the collector who bought a selection while they were to be had. One such collector is Lee Felbinger of Green Lane, Pennsylvania. Felbinger is a collector of Lone Ranger memorabilia, with a collection that today spans over a half-century of mementoes of the Masked Rider of the Plains. "The 1981 film, *The Legend of the Lone Ranger* was a box office flop," Felbinger said, "but a great many of the items which were licensed and distributed were first class and are highly collectable." Added to the film's lukewarm reception were additional complications, Felbinger said. "Due to problems in the production of

the movie, the opening date was postponed six months. Many of the manufacturers were disappointed and gave many of the products a very limited shelf life. " He also explained that distribution of

Lone Ranger storybook.

Lone Ranger pop-out book in action.

*Lone Ranger and Silver
action figures.*

products from the film was very poor in some portions of the country, particularly the Midwest. Felbinger said that in view of these factors, he felt merchandise produced for *The Legend of the Lone Ranger* will be among "the most valuable collectibles of the 1980s."

The Lone Ranger specialist's research on the film has resulted in a list of some 100 different items that were produced specifically for the movie, of which he has personally acquired about ninety-five. Among the items he now owns is a *Legend of the Lone Ranger* game made by Milton Bradley; a sixty-five-piece Lone Ranger western play set manufactured by H. G. Indus-

tries; a Lone Ranger "Ride On Silver" inflatable horse produced by Carlin Playthings; a Lone Ranger pop-up book published by Random House; Lone Ranger Halloween costume and mask manufactured by Ben Cooper; a rare Lone Ranger beach towel made by Barth and Dreyfuss of California; Lone Ranger and Tonto underwear made by Union Underwear Company; assorted belt buckles, a record, lunch box, party horns, and more. He said that some of these latest Lone Ranger items are "already commanding big prices in the collectibles field." Felbinger said that the market for Lone Ranger items, no matter what the vintage, remains strong. Indeed, original premiums dating from the days the Lone Ranger and Tonto roamed the great radio prairie can today bring prices anywhere from $35 to $175—clever items like the movie ring (with pictures of the Lone Ranger), flashlight ring, and secret compartment ring.

Return to Oz

Collectors appear to have assumed a "so what if it bombed" attitude regarding Disney Studio's *Return To Oz*, a film that showed no measurable return at the ticket window when it was released in

1985. Most of the 2000 members comprising The International Wizard of Oz Club loved it just the same, and out of it came many desirable collectibles, as well. That's the word from Oziana collector Fred Meyer of Escanaba, Michigan. Meyer is a columnist for *The Baum Bugle*, the club's official publication dedicated to the creations of L. Frank Baum, author of the Oz books. I contacted Meyer late in 1985, and at that time he was expressing the lament felt by many Oz buffs that *Return to Oz* had fizzled. "Last summer at the Oz convention one of the first questions asked was, 'Did you see the movie?'" he said. "Most had seen it at least once and some had seen it more than once." And what was his assessment of the Disney effort? "Generally, I liked the film, but I am sure that the 1939 movie will remain secure in the affections of all of us." Another Oz buff, Jean Nelson, who runs a shop called The Yellow Brick Road, in Chesterton, Indiana, told me that she felt "it was a shame that *Return to Oz* got so many bad reviews. What's funny to me is the fact that so did the original MGM movie, *The Wizard of Oz*, when it came out in 1939." She said that a series of books produced for the Disney film, which she carried in her shop, "sold out quickly." She sees a welcome place for *Return to Oz* memorabilia in the hands of serious Oziana buffs. "You can be sure that Oz collectors will buy anything Oz," she said. Meanwhile, Fred Meyer has put together a list of the items he and other collectors are aware of being spun off the film. "Exactly how great interest is in collecting the *Return to Oz* collectibles is not yet clear," he remarked, "but a good many of us have at least some items." His list includes Little Golden Books, a paper doll book, game, puzzles, calendar, hand puppets (promoted by Smucker's jam), and stickers. "Rumor has it that in Canada there are Tik-Tok clock and Jack Pumpkinhead lamps [bearing the names of two Baum characters featured in the Disney film], but I have not seen them so I can't say if they really exist," Meyer said.

Beaver's Back

The mining of the past is a trend not confined to the big screen only during the '80s. The decade witnessed that favorite among '60s TV families, the Cleavers, returning to our living rooms in the form of a CBS two-hour made-for-television movie called "Still the

Beaver." In their new incarnation, the Cleavers were depicted as "coping with the problems of the 1980s." Beaver was now a paunchy divorced father in his thirties and Wally was fighting impotence. The Cleavers eventually moved to the Disney Channel, where they lasted about a season. Some new Beaver items surfaced during the Beaver revival: Beaver buttons, a line of trading cards marketed by Pacific Trading Cards of Edmonds, Washington, showing black and white scenes from the old "Leave It To Beaver" series, and boxes of Kellogg's Corn Flakes sporting a contemporary picture of Tony Dow as Wally and Jerry Mathers as the Beaver.

And Other Old and New Favorites

The television neighborhood has changed quite a bit

"Leave it to Beaver"
pinback and trading cards.

since the Beav's heyday. While we allowed ourselves to be occasionally immersed in nostalgia, the rash of reunion shows couldn't hold a candle in the Nielson households when compared to those rating powerhouses, the nighttime soaps. "Dallas" kicked the door open to the genre early in the decade and for a while J.R. Ewing merchandise flourished, including "J.R. Ewing for President" buttons, distributed by a California outfit called One Stop, and cans of J.R. Beer, especially brewed by the Pearl Brewing Company of San Antonio. It would take a lot of J.R. Beer, however, to convince many folks to fork over the cash needed to buy the ultimate in TV collectibles of the '80s, the showcase Alexis and Krystle "Dynasty" dolls marketed by Fine Art Acquisitions and World Doll Inc. Nice dolls, but a bit pricey. They sold for $10,000 apiece and were limited to a production run of ten each when introduced in February 1985. Cheapskates were able to buy the 18-inch vinyl World Doll versions for $100 per doll. About the same time, Royal Orleans was unveiling its new "Dynasty" limited edition collector plate series, painted by artist Shell Fisher. Their initial price: $35 per plate.

Royal Orleans' "Dynasty" plate was a direct response to its earlier success in bringing popular television programs into the collector plate market. One of its first successes came in 1982 when the New Orleans-based producer issued a plate titled "M*A*S*H—The Commemorative Plate." In announcing the plate in August of that year, Royal Orleans said that "this plate will be produced only during the calendar year 1983," the same year that saw the final season for the long-running CBS series. "At year's end production artwork and tools will be destroyed," the company promised. Each $25 plate was serially numbered and came in a "camouflage" gift box. Television's place in our heritage was perhaps most dramatically emphasized when the

J.R. beer can produced by the Pearl Brewing Company.

Smithsonian Institution announced that same year that its Museum of American History was opening a special exhibit of props and other artifacts culled from "M*A*S*H"'s eleven-year run on television. Displayed in the same building housing Old Glory and George Washington's teeth were a dress worn by "Klinger" (Jamie Farr), the "Swamp" (which figured prominently into the show), the infamous liquor still, and the familiar signpost denoting the distances between the fictitious medical compound and places like Burbank and Coney Island. The Smithsonian arranged to have the series' stars Alan Alda ("Hawkeye") and Mike Farrell ("B.J.") on hand for the July 29 opening of the exhibit. What they didn't anticipate was the size of the crowd that would come to see the exhibit. More than 17,000 fans coverged on the premises during the first week alone. In the end, the "M*A*S*H" exhibit attracted more people to the Smithsonian than any other display in its history. At the same time, it became something of a tidy little profit center for the museum. Tons of "M*A*S*H" souvenirs were sold at a specially set up booth in the main entranceway of the museum, dispensing ev-

erything from toy ambulances, T-shirts, tote bags to personalized dog tags for top dollar prices.

Tips for TV Collecting

What's the best television collectible to be had for the least amount of investment year after year? Pop culturists might tell you that it's a copy of *TV Guide*. There are collectors in this country who have saved every copy of *TV Guide* since the national magazine first appeared in 1953. If you don't have access to the corner of an airplane hangar in which to stockpile copies, here are a few points to remember while rummaging through the pile of back issues out in the garage, according to *TV Guide* collectors:

Keep the Fall Preview edition, as it is traditionally a favorite with TV collectors. Also popular are the *TV Guide* editions with covers featuring Presidents or members of their family (Jimmy Carter, Ronald Reagan and Nancy Reagan have all appeared on the cover of *TV Guide* this decade),

Special televised news events (the Royal Wedding),

Superstars no longer with us (John Lennon, Elvis Presley),

Major sports events (Los Angeles Olympics).

The least desirable copies seem to be those that feature television stars. Some will break away from the pack, specifically those from the top-rated series: the cast of

"Dallas," "Dynasty," "The Cosby Show," "Hill Street Blues," "Cheers," "Family Ties," "Miami Vice," among them. Chances are each of these programs will be on the tube, being rerun, somewhere, twenty years from now.

A Salad Dressing to Save

Like anything, the recognition factor is important in affixing levels of desirability to memorabilia, whether it be the cover of a television magazine or on the label of a new line of salad dressing. Take for example what happened when Paul Newman decided in 1982 to market his own brand of salad dressing, called "Newman's Own"—an olive oil and vinegar dressing created by the actor himself. When bottles of the dressing first hit the shelf of a leading dairy store in Norwalk, Connecticut, people grabbed them up by the armfuls. Even taking into consideration the local infatuation with Newman (he and his wife, Joanne Woodward, live next door in Westport), the fact that Stew Leonard's was cleaned out of 10,000 bottles in three weeks' time is impressive by any standard. Brisk sales of Newman's Own were soon being reported by other Northeas-

Paul Newman's Own salad dressing.

tern supermarkets. As the *Boston Globe* pointed out at the time, "The label features a picture of the actor that will make every unit a collector's item if the demand turns out to be just a fad." *The Baltimore Evening Sun* reported that while Newman's Own was supposed to retail for between $1.19 to $1.39 a bottle, it was turning up in Baltimore specialty food shops for as much as $1.79. At a press conference in New York, where the salad dressing was first introduced, reviews for Newman's concoction were mixed. A food editor from New Jersey called it "delicate," while a reporter from Connecticut equated it with something you'd expect to be served in a high school cafeteria. The salad dressing was soon followed up by a Paul Newman spaghetti sauce, and both products sold quite well. Empty salad dressing bottles now turn up at flea markets priced between $8 to $10 in the oddball cinemabilia category, proving once and for all that it's not what's in a salad dressing that makes it good, but rather the degree of hoopla which goes into making it.

The 1980s also turned out to be the salad days for another movie star. His name is Ronald Reagan.

7. Politics

Ronald Reagan

What happens to prices for a former movie star's screen memorabilia once that person becomes President of the United States? In the case of Ronald Reagan, prices for items from his old films went right through the ceiling. "They're still rising," said Rene Parenteau, president of the Reagan Political Items Collectors (Rt. 1, Box 258-B, Denison, TX 75020). For years, Reaganiana collected dust in the corner of movie memorabilia shops. Except in California, where he served as governor for two terms, Reagan cinemabilia fell far short of the going prices for comparable artifacts from films starring many other actors on the Warner Brothers lot—the Humphrey Bogarts and Jimmy Cagneys. "After he ran for the Republican nomination and lost to Gerald Ford in 1976, you could buy most large Reagan posters for between $20 and $25," Parenteau said. The Texas man, who began accumulating political memorabilia in 1968, had great faith in the perseverance of Ronald Wilson Reagan, however. "I know that someday he'd make it all the way to the White House," he said. Between 1976 and 1978, Parenteau acquired most of the 150 Reagan movie posters now in his collection. When Ronald Reagan won the Presidency in 1980, Parenteau's patience was rewarded: his posters increased in value tenfold overnight. All over America, owning an authentic Reagan film poster became the ultimate status symbol. In December 1980, *The Wall Street Journal* reported that Los Angeles and Washington, D. C., collectibles dealers were selling scarce 22-inch by 28-inch posters from Reagan's 1951 comedy, *Bedtime For Bonzo* in which he played second banana to a chimpanzee. The poster, which depicted the newly elected President of the United States standing on his head, went for $450, while a one-sheet poster from Reagan's first film, *Love Is On The Air*, now commanded $800. The inflated prices of the post-election euphoria didn't begin to come back down to earth until the following summer.

Of Reagan's fifty-three films, made between 1937 to his last film in 1964 (*The Kill-*

ers), the bulk today sell for between $150 and $250. "If you want to buy one of his early film posters from the '30s today, you're talking about paying $400 to $500 in most cases," Parenteau explained. They are very desirable items, which continue to find their market. "I'd love to get my hands on a few in particular myself," the Reagan buff said.

Reagan's screen days became immediate grist for parodies, which were rushed onto the market after his accension to the highest office in the land. One of the best was a product of the Eighty-Two Corporation of Boston: an 18-by-27-inch *Bedtime For Brezhnev* poster, "starring" Ronald Reagan. Reagan is depicted on the poster in white hat, collaring a black-hatted Leonid Brezhnev. With Nancy at his side, Mr. Reagan's supporting cast included sidekick George Bush, General Alexander Haig (dressed in a cavalry uniform), and Henry Kissinger as "Doc." A teaser on the poster reads, "From out of the west, they dusted off their guns . . . to protect the world they knew and the women they loved!" The Reagan era was obviously under way.

Rene Parenteau reports that about 40 percent of the members of the Reagan Political

Ronald Reagan book for children.

Items Collectors include Reagan movie memorabilia in their stockpiles. The remaining 60 percent concentrate on acquiring items from Mr. Reagan's political career. These range from collectors who have a smattering of buttons from the 1980 and '84 campaigns to a Reagan buff in Oakland, California ("far and away the biggest collector," Parenteau vouched), who counts practically every button ever produced bearing Reagan's name among a collection that embraces over 1000 individual pieces of Reaganiana. "There were far more items produced during the 1984 campaign than can be found from the '80 election," Parenteau said. The rea-

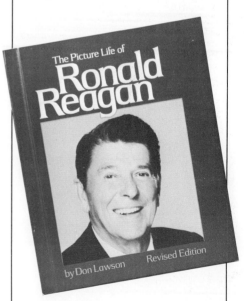

95

son, he explained, was Mr. Reagan's immense popularity during the '84 election, which netted the President a landslide reelection. "So many more people were for him in '84 that more items were made to meet the demand." He also said that Reagan's popularity figured into a great number of so-called "coattail" buttons produced during the 1984 election. "Republican candidates from nearly every state came out with buttons bearing their name and Reagan's, trying to ride on his coattails," Parenteau explained.

One of the most popular buttons from the '84 campaign is actually an anti-Mondale

Ronald Reagan "Dutch" chocolate ice cream.

pin. "It is a takeoff of the film, *Ghostbusters*," Parenteau said, "called 'Fritzbusters.' " The button was modeled after similar pins released to promote the 1984 film, which showed a cartoon of a ghost with a void symbol superimposed. "The ghost on the 'Fritzbusters' buttons resembled Mondale." The pins were a big hit at the Republican National Convention in Dallas that year, marketed in various sizes, including one priced at $25. "The 6-inch-diameter one now goes for about $10," Parenteau said. Another popular button at the convention appeared to be a typical Reagan-Bush pin at first glance. This pin, however, came equipped with a built-in battery. "It was a music button which had a couple of flashing lights on it and played the 'Star Spangled Banner.' It could go for a hundred-some-odd hours without stopping."

After Reagan's election, collectors began combing his boyhood hometown of Dixon, Illinois, looking for unique souvenirs of the fortieth President of the United States. Among the treasures to be had were half-gallon size ice cream cartons produced for a brand of Dutch chocolate ice cream made by the Hey Brothers Ice Cream Company of Dixon

"Honoring Dixon's Ronald 'Dutch' Reagan." Each carton carried a drawing of the house on Hennepin Avenue where "Dutch" (Reagan's boyhood nickname) lived between 1920 and 1924. Dixon also contributed another collectible to the annals of Reaganabilia when collectors around the country flooded the offices of the *Dixon Evening Telegraph* with requests for its November 5, 1980 edition, reporting on the hometown boy's victory. The newspaper had to go back on press to meet the demand, with one local dealer buying up 5000 copies alone for subsequent sales at premium prices.

Doodles by Ronald Reagan.

It is the cheaper-priced items that are enjoying the greatest popularity with members of the Reagan collectors club. "We are mostly blue-collar workers and can't afford the expensive items," the group's president explained. Yet, higher priced items were being marketed even before Reagan took the oath of office for the first time. These ranged from inaugural collector plates, such as a $50 porcelain plate carrying portraits of Reagan and Bush painted by Douglas Van Howd and produced by Wildlife Art., Ltd—Heritage Americana Series, to Ronald Reagan character jugs that originally sold for $500. The latter limited-edition jugs were made by Royal Doulton and commissioned by the Republican National Committee in 1984 in an edition of 2000 and sold to benefit the James S. Brady Presidential Foundation. Royal Doulton character jugs of world leaders enjoy a good track record. Among the rarest and most valuable is a 1940 edition shaped in the likeness of Winston Churchill. The value of this piece now stands at around $10,000.

In 1982, Herman Darvick, president of the Universal Autograph Collectors Club (P.O. Box 467, Rockville Centre, New York 11571), told me that Ronald Reagan writes and signs more handwritten notes than any other President in this century. Like John Kennedy before him, President Reagan is an occasional doodler. Notes for his speeches are often embellished with facial caricatures; cowboys, sailors, and wavy-haired women are among his specialties. The President has been known to doodle during Cabinet meetings and on occasion presents the product of his idle pen to Cabinet members and other administration oficials. These items, Reagan watchers say, may prove to be among the hottest mementoes of the Reagan years. The reason, according to Darvick, is that they are drawn on White House stationery. "The White House stationery is the most official stationery in the whole world and for that reason these drawings have a great potential value." A sheet of Reagan doodles could be expected to fetch $1500 to $2000 on the collecting market during the Reagan Administration, Darvick estimated. That price should increase drastically in coming years, as the Reagan era enters the history books.

Parenteau of the Reagan Political Items Collectors said that members of his club also

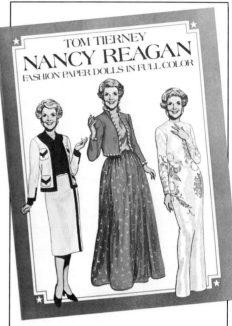

Nancy Reagan paper doll book.

provide a warm welcome to Nancy Reagan collectibles. The most popular of these date back to Mrs. Reagan's own film days, when she was known as Nancy Davis. "Collectors are especially interested in posters from the movie *Hellcats of the Navy*," he said, referring to the film in which the future First Lady co-starred with her husband. Of contemporary interest is the Nancy Reagan fashion paper doll book, published in 1983 by Dover Publications, Inc., of New York and retailing at the time for $3.50. The book featured one cut-out doll and thirty-one fashions drawn by illustrator Tom Tierney. The selection included a black-and-silver "starfish" gown and a white square-dancing dress of crinkle cotton ("worn at her fifty-eighth birthday barbecue," we are told).

Jimmy Carter

While collectibles from the Reagan administration continued to appear during the President's second term, the man he defeated in 1980, Jimmy Carter, is already finding a comfortable niche in the collecting hall of fame. When it comes to which campaign offers the best prizes, the opposite situation to Reagan's prevails with Carter: memorabilia from his first Presidential campaign in 1976 is much more abundant than that produced for the 1980 election. "The wide array and selections of Carter memorabilia that existed from all the hoopla in 1976 wasn't present in his reelection campaign," said A. Neil LeDock, president of the Carter Political Items Collectors (P.O. Box 1414, Decatur, Georgia 30030), a specialty chapter of the American Political Items Collectors. "Obviously, his unpopularity with the public at the time, the Iranian hostage crisis, and the brutal inner party struggle with the Kennedy faction all led to a downturn in reelection

memorabilia both in the range of items available and the amount produced." Consequently, Carter connoisseurs remember 1976 as "a great year," when there were "more buttons issued for Jimmy Carter than ever issued for a single candidate in one election," LeDock said. The '76 campaign saw a great many peanut-related Carter items produced—the most popular items to Carter collectors. LeDock said that the peanut theme was all but abandoned in 1980. One peanut-related item, billed as dating from the '80 campaign, was a walking

Jimmy Carter walking peanut.

windup novelty showing President Carter in the shape of a peanut and measuring five inches high. An outfit called the Last Wound-Up Inc., of New York was still advertising these as a "warehouse find" in collecting journals late in 1985, for $10 each.

"Among the 1980 items that Carter collectors deem desirable are campaign buttons, posters (especially those announcing a visit), some paper items and ribbons, which are in scarce supply and start at $10 each today, if you are lucky enough to find one," Le-Dock explained. He went on to say that 1980 buttons start at a dollar or two and seldom exceed $50. "Carter did not undertake extensive campaigning, due to the crisis in Iran, and this cut drastically down on buttons issued by local Democrats." Those that do exist from the election command top dollar, as "these types of buttons are the ones that bring the higher prices in more modern times." Roger Van Sickle of Delaware, Ohio, who is the national secretary of the Carter Political Items Collectors, has collected Carter memorabilia since 1975. He said that Carter-Mondale jugate buttons (portraying both the Presidential and Vice-Presidential candidates) and specific state buttons will bring the best prices in the future. "Some states produced small quantities, where the National Headquarters produced buttons in great masses," Van Sickle said. "So state buttons are in great demand." The national buttons were largely produced by N.G. Slater of New York and the Trimble Co. of Pittsburgh, while the state buttons are identified on the bottom of the button as to the state of their origin and carry a Union mark. "National Carter and Mondale buttons could range between $3 to $5, while a state button from Alaska, for example, could be valued at $40 to $45," Van Sickle pointed out.

Van Sickle said one button that is a favorite with Carter buffs features a cartoon of Carter riding a donkey with a whip aiming toward rival Democrat aspirant Ted Kennedy. The button reads "If Kennedy runs, I'll whip his ass." Variations of this remark, made by Carter during the heat of the election, showed up on buttons as well as posters. While collector LeDock prices examples in his collection between $2 to $5 at the present time, he said that "many collectors feel that this may earn the distinction of becoming a classic." Van Sickle said that buttons from the 1980 Democratic convention reflect the mood of many of the delegates. One carried the words "Democratic Showdown," he said, and pictured Carter and Kennedy. Another one, made in Eugene, Oregon, asked "How Is the 1980 Democratic National Convention Like a Mount St. Helens Volcano?" "Rarely seen, this button refers to the explosive nature of the Democratic National Convention," LeDock said. A little sack attached to the bottom of the pin contained what was reputed to be actual volcanic dust from Mount St. Helens. LeDock prices it at between $6 and $8, but feels that it is one of the era's

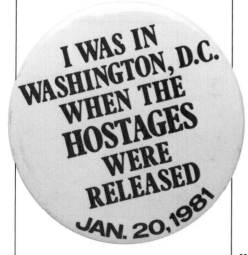

Hostages pinback buttons.

"sleepers" which will someday command high prices.

The Iranian hostage situation, which many feel cut greatly into Carter's chances for reelection, turns up on many Carter collectibles. Iranian Hostage buttons in their own right are turning up at flea markets with hefty price tags. I bought one from a sidewalk vendor in Washington, D.C., in 1984; it was already over three years old when I got my hands on it. It reads: "I Was In Washington, D.C., When the Hostages Were Released Jan. 20, 1981." I paid $8 for it. Another one, which I picked up the same year for $10, was made by N. G. Slater and carried the words "Welcome Home Hostages, Free At Last, Jan. 20, 1981, 444 Days." A yellow ribbon attached to the bottom of the button carried the message "Welcome Home To Freedom." Two hostage buttons in the LeDock collection reflect the frustration and ultimate relief associated with the long ordeal. One pin shows a cartoon of the Ayatollah Khomeni behind bars and reads "Unite America, Support Pres. Carter." The second, issued after the hostages gained their release on the very day Ronald Regan was being sworn into office, stated "America Thanks You, Jimmy,

52 Times," referring to the fifty-two hostages who were released. LeDock anticipates that these buttons will rise appreciably in value in the years to come.

Objects, while not plentiful, do turn up from the '80 Carter campaign. Van Sickle said that one item that has already more than doubled in value is a limited edition knife made by the Case Knife Co. "They made an edition for Carter and Reagan," he said. The Carter knife is of medium size and white, showing a donkey and reading "Carter 1980." "It sold for $15 to the collector when new and now brings $35 or more on the market." Another object of interest is a Jimmy Carter watch, produced by Genova in '80, showing Carter riding a donkey. "It is very colorful and came on a leather strap," Van Sickle explained. He said that when new, it sold for $20, now fetches about $10 more, and is well on its way to becoming a "top dollar" item in the Carter collecting field.

Both Van Sickle and LeDock stressed the potential future worth of Carter's autographed memorabilia. "An average Carter signature will bring $100 to $125," Van Sickle said. "I might caution collectors on autographs—some letters on White House stationery could be signed by an autopen" (a mechanical device that affixes a remarkably close facsimile of one's signature). "Also, it was a known fact that his secretary signed, also. A collector must have a good eye when collecting such signatures." He said that since leaving the Presidency, "most, if not all," Carter signatures have been authentic. Among these are the inscribed editions of President Carter's memoirs, *Keeping Faith* (1983). There were three editions of the book, said LeDock. The first one is a leather-bound affair that sold for $300, while the second, a deluxe edition that came in a blue slipcase, priced at $60. Both of these were of limited editions and personally signed by Mr. Carter. (The third edition was the standard hardcover copy, which was sold without a signature.) LeDock said the signed editions are sought not only by political collectors but autograph and book collectors as well. "I have already been offered $125 for my $60 edition," he attested. LeDock expects prices for these signed editions to "soar in years to come."

Because LeDock owns what is considered the largest private collection of Carter memorabilia in the country, people often ask him what they should do with their Carter trinkets and the like. "I tell them to hold on to them," he said, without hesitation. "Carter values downturned drastically following his perceived 'failure' as a President. Part of this is natural, as happens with all candidates after the euphoria dies down from an election campaign." He said that only now has interest in Carter memorabilia ceased bottoming out and is "slowly rising." LeDock expressed his unflagging interest in Carter collectibles by saying, "Most political pundits feel that history will be kinder to Jimmy Carter and for this reason I'm bullish on his memorabilia. I draw a parallel to Harry Truman, who narrowly won the office on his own in 1948 and who was so unpopular that he declined to run again in 1952. But these days, he is considered to have been one of our best Presidents; his memorabilia brings high prices and are highly sought after by collectors." LeDock is sure that "Carter's time will come," too, and in anticipation he continues his quest for buttons, banners, ribbons, and such recalling the political career of the man from Plains, Georgia.

Predicting Future Collectibles

In the game of speculation about political memorabilia, one's ability to foretell the ultimate course of the political winds counts for everything. Years in advance of elections, collectors are writing to hotshot Senators and members of the Congress requesting autographs in the hope that someday fate will find these men heading a winning ticket that will take them all the way to the White House. "Collectors are constantly trying to second-guess history and accumulate memorabilia from likely candidates for the Presidency before the rush diminishes the supply," according to Joseph Hayes of San Antonio, the secretary treasurer for the American Political Items Collectors. "For example, if Walter Mondale had been elected President in 1984, all of his Congressional buttons from the past would have suddenly become valuable. That happened to Jimmy Carter's buttons from his days as the Governor of Georgia when he was elected in '76."

History has also shown that bigtime losers can return some day to become winners, as evidenced by the return of Richard Nixon after his 1960 defeat to John Kennedy, or

Ronald Reagan's comeback four years after losing his party's nomination to incumbent Gerry Ford in '76. One candidate who many people refuse to give up on is Ted Kennedy. Kennedy memorabilia continues to ride the hills and valleys of political fortunes during each campaign, as speculation persists in some quarters that Ted will someday reside at 1600 Pennsylvania Avenue. Kennedy memorabilia, most of it dating from his unsuccessful 1980 campaign, was riding high through most of 1985 in expectation that he would soon announce his second run for the Presidency. The bot-

tom fell out, however, on December 18 of that year when he announced that he would not run for President, but instead direct his efforts to maintaining his position in the U.S. Senate. Yet, Kennedy's powerful position in twentieth-century politics asssures that his memorabilia will always find a place in the collecting field, whether or not he ever occupies the White House. His 1980 campaign, in fact, was responsible for a most humorous by-product: a 1980 version of the venerable Teddy Bear. As just about everybody knows, the Teddy Bear's origin is purely politi-

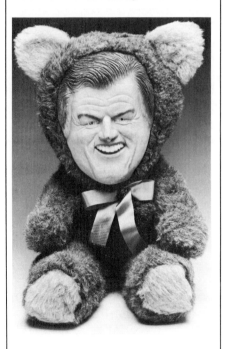

Teddy Kennedy and Ronnie bears.

cal; it was so named, in the first years of this century, after Teddy Roosevelt. It seemed only natural to retiree Wes Soderstrom of Woodland Hills, California, that when this century's other Teddy announced that he was running for President in 1980, it was time to bring back the political Teddy Bear. And back it came, for $49.50 a pop, bearing the face of the senator from Massachusetts. Soderstrom's Teddy Bears were marketed largely through advertisements placed in national collecting publications. When Ronald Reagan won the election, Soderstrom emerged with another bear in time for the '81 inauguration: the Ronnie bear, followed in 1982 with the Nancy bear. "These bears have never been distributed in large numbers, but their future desirability by serious collectors—due to their rarity and uniqueness—seems already assured," Soderstrom told me. He explained that the bears are American-made and the remarkably lifelike faces are the result of a complex process he has developed. He begins with an original sculpture, from which the soft vinyl faces are manufactured. Each face is individually painted by airbrush. "Some of the Kennedy Bears were presented to

Politicards were a hit of '84 campaign.

Ted Kennedy by various means," Soderstrom said, "which not surprisingly he never acknowledged. A lady wrote to me that she had presented a Ronnie Bear to President Reagan at a party in New Orleans and that it became the first Teddy Bear ever to fly on Air Force One." He later sent a companion Nancy Bear to the President and "I received a very nice letter from him thanking me and my family."

No one knows, however, whether any of the candidates in the '84 election wound up playing solitaire with a deck of Politicards, Inc., but the novelty hit of that summer dealt a profit for the Washington-based outfit, which produced 25,000 of them that year. The cards received the distinction of being given the "New Deal Award" in a column appearing in *USA Today*. The newspaper called Politicards "the most clever souvenir on the streets. The pricey ($10) deck of playing cards features caricatures of such pols as Geraldine Ferraro in a tiger-striped body suit and George Bush in a wind-up tux."

The big winner that summer, however, would also turn out to be that year's big loser, Walter "Fritz" Mondale. Hayes of the American Political Items Collectors felt that Mondale's claim to fame in the political memorabilia field will be as

John Glenn pinback button.

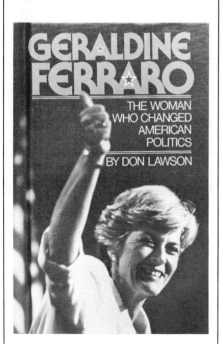

Geraldine Ferraro book for children.

the guy on the button with the first woman Vice-Presidential candidate. "The Mondale material which will be of the greatest future interest will be those in which he is pictured with Geraldine Ferraro," he said. These include jugate buttons as well as posters. "I know that posters showing the two of them were fairly scarce in some parts of the country," Hayes said. While few Mondale buttons were distributed during the campaign compared to the enormous cavalcade of Reagan pins, there were enough of them so that the national pins at the present time hold little worth. "A lot of Mondale collectors went after the individual state pins made by the unions," he said. Again, it is those in which Ferraro is mentioned or, better yet, shown which are the most popular, because of the historic "first" such pins imply.

The strong emergence of Jessie Jackson during the primary also would indicate an important place for Jackson memorabilia in any political collection of the '80s. But finding Jackson memorabilia will not be easy, as I can personally attest to. In January 1984, I was in southern New Hampshire. This was just a few weeks before the first-in-the-

JACKSON
84

"A just society,
a peaceful
world."

*Jesse Jackson handout
flyer.*

nation primary held in the state and, as could have been predicted, would-be Presidents were crisscrossing the snowcovered hills in search of voters. Meanwhile, I was busying myself trying to scoop up as many political buttons as possible, knowing full well that once the primaries got under way, the pack of hopefuls would diminish dramatically. I carried out my search for souvenirs at rallies and campaign headquarters at the state capital. In short order, I had a small cargo ship of Reagan material, a goodly number of Mondale pins and bumper

stickers, as well as political paraphernalia expounding the virtues of John Glenn, Ernest Hollings, George McGovern, Alan Cranston, Gary Hart, and even Reuben Askew—all free for the asking. Only Jesse Jackson items (short of one, a rainbow-colored flyer) evaded my attention—and this at a time when Jackson's visibility was high in the state. I finally tracked down a bonafide Jackson pin being sold at the entrance table at a Jackson Rally held in a school auditorium in Keene, New Hampshire. The pins were being sold for $2 apiece and carried the images of Jackson, an eagle, the Capitol dome, and a rainbow (symbolizing Jackson's "Rainbow Coalition"). Printed on the button were the words "Win, Jesse, Win, President in 1984." It was explained to me

*Jesse Jackson pinback
button.*

107

that Mr. Jackson's campaign chest was running low and consequently buttons were being sold rather than given away.

One thing is important to remember in the field of political memorabilia: there are always a lot more losers than winners. And with a fresh crop of losers joining the ranks of political footnotes after each election, candidates will try anything to gain attention. If the money is there, they will often attempt to stand out in the crowd via their campaign material. Attractive buttons or a catchy campaign design can create this effect. And collectors love interesting buttons. As Joseph Hayes pointed out, Alf Landon for President buttons from 1936 are very valuable, in some cases fetching over $1000 today. And it is not because Landon is remembered as having gone down to a crushing defeat at the hands of Franklin Roosevelt. It is because Landon's buttons, which featured sunflowers, are pretty to look at. The best rule of thumb during any campaign year is to go with your instincts. If you have an opportunity to acquire a button that appears to be extraordinary in any way, disregard for a moment how far down on the polls its namesake may pres-

Orwell presidential campaign pinback.

ently stand. If the button is visually appealing or, even better, if it flashes, buzzes, sings, changes colors, or does anything else an ordinary button wouldn't be expected to do, buy it. It's a safe bet that it is a limited-production item which will enjoy a rosy future regardless of its candidate's political success or failure.

The Fun Stuff

No decade would be complete without its share of wacko Presidential candidates, and during the '80s they didn't come much wackier than the day in April 1984 when a committee announced the Presidential candidacy of George Orwell, the author of the book *Nineteen Eighty-Four.* Never mind the fact that Mr. Orwell had been dead for over thirty years and his descendants wanted nothing to do with the affair. Stephen G. Silverman, president of the Orwell National Committee, figured that the day at last had come for the creator of Big Brother—and all you had to do was look at the calendar to know that. Silverman, thirty-three, along with his brother, Richard, twenty-nine, and cousin Jay, also twenty-nine, dreamed up the scheme and counted on the mass-interest in Orwell that would be forthcoming as the world approached the real 1984. Every national news magazine would mention Orwell and one in particular, *Harper's,* would even put him on their cover. Meanwhile, a new edition of his book, first published in 1949, was being readied for press, with a preface by Walter Cronkite. Even taking all this into consideration, it's still a puzzlement that the Silvermans of Lancaster, Pennsylvania, would go to all the effort of financing one of the most obscure political campaigns to come down the pike. The Silvermans said in their

press package, issued that year, "Our interest in mounting this campaign is solely to build awareness and sales for a line of products relating to themes suggested in Mr. Orwell's book." The Silvermans, it turns out, had something to sell—a lot of things, to be precise. Adopting fire-engine red for the color of their product line, they produced merchandise that made use of two catch phrases: "Big Brother Is Watching You" and "Elect George Orwell President." Sold by mail order and in book and general merchandise stores, the products included a poster and calendar ($3.50 each), bumper stickers ($1.50), buttons ($1), T-shirts ($7.95), and a pair of nifty $5 stoneware mugs that would have pleased even the pessimistic Mr. Orwell. In the end, Orwell lost, but the Silvermans had found a place in the field of obscuriana.

Out of the Past

During the 1980s, anniversaries brought the names of three former Chief Executives back into prominence and along with it reevalutions of their eras: the centennial of Franklin Roosevelt's birth, the twentieth anniversary of President Kennedy's assassination, and the tenth anniver-

George Orwell for President mug, pinback, and bumper sticker.

media. *Newsweek*'s cover featured a black-and-white photo of Kennedy with the words "What JFK Meant to Us." *Time*'s cover, featuring a windswept painting of the young President, asked: "J.F.K. How Good a President Was He?" *TV Guide* the same week ran a Richard Amsel painting of John and Jacqueline.

Bonnie Gardner has been watching the Kennedy legend for many years now; she is president of the Kennedy Political Items Collectors (1337 Olivine, Mentone, CA 92359). I asked her what items from the twentieth-anniversary period are deemed worthy of adding to her collection, and before answering, she conferred with several other leading Kennedy collectors for a consensus of thought. "All of us kept the magazines with cover stories on President Kennedy that were issued in November of 1983," Gardner said. "We look at these as having historical significance. The very fact that there were so many cover stories commemorating the twentieth anniversary is of considerable significance. There were also a significant number of video materials that surfaced or resurfaced in November 1983." She said that commemorative materials came from some unexpect-

sary of Richard Nixon's quagmire, Watergate. As is the case with such observances, each dominated the printed and electronic media during the week of the anniversary (ABC devoted one entire evening of primetime television to a three-hour special tracing the life of FDR), while a rush of new books on the former Presidents hit the book stalls. Each also created a burst of new collectibles.

The twentieth anniversary of the Kennedy assassination in November 1983 brought forth a gush of Camelot from the

ed quarters. Among these was a black-and-white pinback button produced in two sizes, 2 1/4 inches and 6 inches by the Bellmar Junior High School of Belle Vernon, Pennsylvania, in connection with a special J.F.K. assembly it held. "There is also a button-ribbon combination, but I do not know the history of the item," said Gardner. "The ribbon reads 'Collins' Bar and Grill,' pictures a U.S. flag, and reads '20th Anniversary of John F. Kennedy, Nov. 22, 1963, Nov. 22, 1983.'"

While the marking of the Kennedy assassination spawned a few collectibles on a grassroots level, the centennial of FDR's birth in January 1982 was an event that produced artifacts in some pretty high places, not the least of which

Kennedy pinback produced on 20th anniversary of his assassination.

FDR centennial poster.

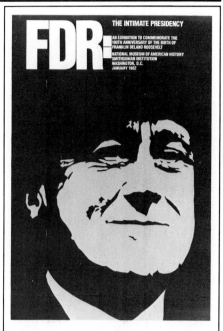

was at the Smithsonian. The institution mounted a special exhibition that year called "FDR, The Intimate Presidency," dealing with Roosevelt and the mass media in the 1930s. Among the merchandise to come out of the exhibit was a particularly stunning poster designed by Gilbert Lesser and showing a high-contrast photo of Roosevelt in orange and navy blue.

My favorite anniversary-related item, however, surfaced just in advance of the tenth anniversary of the break-in of the Democratic headquarters at the Watergate in Washington. It is perhaps the best example of the lengths some

FDR centennial booklet.

collectors will go to create a one-of-a-kind collectible. The most important document to come out of the Watergate episode surely must be Richard Nixon's actual letter turning in his resignation as President of the United States. That document is safely under lock and key in the National Archives. In 1981, however, a typed facsimile of the resignation letter, reading, "I hereby resign the Office of President of the United States," and signed by Richard Nixon, turned up for auction at the Charles Hamilton Galleries in New York. It was ultimately purchased by a speculator from Rhode Island for $6250. Less than a week later, the letter was resold for $10,000. While the autograph was authenticated (the letter was actually signed by Mr. Nixon), it is not certain whether he knew what he was signing when he affixed his signature to the paper. Many authorities believe that the former President was simply handed a blank piece of paper to sign by a collector, above which the words copied from the actual resignation letter were later typed. "I believe that the novelty of the item had a lot to do with the high prices it achieved," Herman Darvick of the Universal Autograph Collectors Club told me not long after the sale. It seems that after the original novelty of the item wore off, the value plunged. "A few weeks after the first facsimile letter was sold, another surfaced and was put up for bids by Hamilton," Darvick went on to say. "It brought only $450."

THE WHITE HOUSE

WASHINGTON

August 9, 1974

Dear Mr. Secretary:

I hereby resign the Office of President of the United States.

Sincerely,

The Honorable Henry A. Kissinger
The Secretary of State
Washington, D.C. 20520

Facsimile of Nixon resignation letter.

The Women's Movement

The women's movement inspired some of the items produced during the '80s, although certainly not to the same degree seen during the previous decade, when it first emerged as a political force. A height of activity accompanied the final campaign to gain state ratification of the Equal Rights Amendment (ERA). The showdown came

ERA campaign decals, bumper stickers, pinback.

Suspersisters trading card.

BUFFY SAINTE-MARIE

at the end of June 1982, an event that generated a substantial amount of bumper stickers, banners, brochures, posters, decals, buttons, and other campaignlike items, most of which were produced and distributed by the National Organization of Women (NOW) in Washington. NOW chose green and white as the colors for its materials, which bear for the most part the union emblem of Allied Printing of Washington. New mottos came out of the ERA movement, with "ERA YES" being the most predominant. When ERA failed to gain passage in the additional three states needed for ratification of the Equal Rights Movement, the profusion of ERA material vanished overnight. Wise collectors packed away mementoes of the most recent stage in women's history, documenting one of the lively political moments of an otherwise quiet period on the American political front.

While ERA failed, other developments pertaining to women flourished, including the production and sale of a series of trading cards featuring famous women. Called "Supersisters," the seventy-two-card series was released early in the decade by a New York outfit called Supersisters, Inc., and featured women such as former Senator Margaret Chase Smith, professional skier Susan Chaffee, jet pilot Bonnie Tiburzi, and anthropologist Margaret Mead. Company founder Melissa Rich credits the idea for the cards to her young daughter, who asked her one day why there weren't any girls on trading cards. By late 1981, over 15,000 decks of the cards had been sold at $7.50 a set.

A 1980s bonafide hero was astronaut Sally Ride, who became the first American woman in space when sent aloft with a crew on the Space Shuttle in 1984. During Ride's mission, she carried with her a scarf once belonging to pioneering aviator Amelia Earhart, the first woman to fly across the Atlantic. The scarf was on loan from the National Women's Hall of Fame in Seneca Falls, New York. In October 1985, I contacted Gwendolyn Webber-McLeon, the Hall of Fame's executive director, to ask her what items from the 1980s will someday be sought by historians documenting contemporary women. Her selection includes "copies of *Ms.* magazine, feminist newspapers, various buttons expounding concerns of women (including the Women's Peace Movement), items from the historic Nairobi conference on women, photographs of women in a variety of roles," as well as a pair of "women's running shoes." Prices of women's items being sold at the hall of fame's gift shop range from $35 for a complete set of the fifteen first-day covers honoring famous women during the International Women's Year to $2.95 for a *Great Women Paper Dolls* book, featuring folks like Cleopatra, Joan of Arc, and Florence Nightingale. And here the Susan B. Anthony dollar, that orphan among pocket change, is revered; a collector's edition sells for $10.

8. Sports

Baseball

"Today, the king of collecting is Pete Rose," Allan Kaye, publisher of *Baseball Card News* told *USA Today* in 1983. "If he breaks Cobb's record, I expect the value of his rookie card to go over $1000. On the other hand, if he has a serious injury and misses a major part of the season, or just has a bad year, there's going to be a big drop-off in value. A lot of people are going to take a loss."

No Mudville here; this sports story has a happy ending. The place was Wrigley Field in Chicago. One day in early September 1985, Pete Rose of the Cincinnati Reds caught up with the legendary Ty Cobb's record number of hits, in a game against the Cubs. With two singles, the scoreboard at Wrigley lit up with the historic numbers: ROSE 4191, COBB 4191. Collectors who had been stalking Rose memorabilia for years, just as Rose stalked Cobb, were ecstatic. Their hero had come through. By hit 4192, he left Cobb in the dust and was on his way to sports immortality. And the value of the 1963 Rose rookie card took off for the clouds.

During the '80s, it seemed everything that Rose touched became solid gold and everything that reflects his remarkable career was at least gilded. The rise of Rose is one of this decade's success stories, as evidenced by the price of his rookie card, issued in '63 with a stick of gum; Rose shared the spotlight with four other rookies on the card. Twenty years ago, the card was worth about 10 cents. Even as recently as the late 1970s, when Jim Beckett's *Official Price Guide to Baseball Cards* appeared, the card was listed as worth $5. Then Rose began closing in on history. By 1983, the price had risen to between $350 and $450. The desire to own the card became so great that the inevitable happened: counterfeiters began trying to pass off fake Rose rookie cards. Authorities closed down an operation in southern California that had produced 10,000 bogus Rose rookie cards. Collectors said the counterfeit cards appeared freshly cut, while the real cards' edges feel silky smooth, showing no grain or fiber in the paper. Under a glass, the counterfeits display a dual dot pattern, as opposed to the sharp dots found on original cards of this period. As a result, the fake cards are lacking a fine black line around the letter C on Rose's cap. The line had been broken up by the moire pattern.

There were plenty of legitimate Pete Rose items to go around during the decade, however. The most popular line of goods were produced by Gartlan Associates of Huntington Beach, California. Called the "Pete Rose Platinum Edition," the commemorative series hit the marketplace just as Rose collected hit 4192 and includes five pieces: a collector plate, ceramic baseball cards, ceramic plaque, and porcelain figurine. Only 4192 (get it?) of each item, except for the smaller baseball card, were produced in the edition, with these limited lines personally autographed by Rose himself. The porcelain figurine has Mr. Enthusiasm standing 6 3/4 inches tall on a wooden base and sold for $125. "This masterpiece captures the ever famous batting stance of Rose," a Gartlan promotional piece touted. The $100 plate carried a painting by Ted Sizemore and was titled *The Best of Baseball*. It sports a platinum trim and pictures both

Cobb and Rose.

The idea of putting baseball players on plates actually began with another plate company, Hackett American, when it launched one of the cleverest marketing schemes of the decade: placing a ballplayer on a plate. The company approached Reggie Jackson in 1982 with an offer to reproduce his likeness on 5000 individually numbered plates. Jackson not only embraced the idea, but consented to sign 464 plates for a special "Home Run" series, and a marketing concept was born. The signed Jackson plates were an unqualified success, due in part to the Angels' player's notoriety for refusing to sign autographs. For serious sports fans, here was a way to add Mr. October's autograph

Reggie Jackson collector plate: first of a new genre.

to one's collection—and have a nice piece of "art" to boot. The plates were quickly sold out at $100 apiece. Within a year, they had risen in value to $400. As a result, the company soon released a second baseball superstar plate, this time featuring Steve Garvey of the San Diego Padres. Hackett and Gartlan subsequently put Hank Aaron, Steve Carlton, Gary Carter, Whitey Ford, Dwight Gooden, Willie Mays, Babe Ruth, Nolan Ryan, Tom Seaver, and, of course, Pete Rose, on porcelain. When you're hot, you're hot.

Still, it is baseball cards that remain the number-one collectible in the wide world of sports. The latest figures estimate that 500,000 Americans actively collect baseball cards. And the news in 1982 that the famous Honus Wagner card had just sold for $25,011 certainly didn't hurt the hobby. The bulk of baseball cards remain at their original issue price (the cost of a stick of gum) for a long time, and some never advance much further. One need only consider that the leading producer of baseball cards, Topps Chewing Gum Inc., issues 500 million cards to the public each year. Many collectors feel that the best bet among the multitude of cards in circulation are

Tom Seaver error baseball card.

those picturing today's stars, as well as rookie cards. A hot rookie's card can rapidly appreciate if he's hot when he comes out of the gate. When Fernando Valenzuela excelled during his first season in 1981, his rookie card issued that year soared from two cents to $2 overnight. Bob Lemke, the editor-publisher of *Baseball Cards* magazine out of Iola, Wisconsin, feels that speculating heavily in rookie cards runs too many risks for his dollar. "Too much can happen that can bring the value of a card down—a career-ending injury, for instance," he told me. He admits, however, that the field has its successes. "In

Glenn Hubbard
SECOND BASE

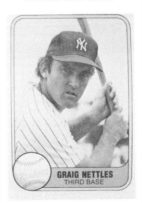

Fleer's Glenn Hubbard card features boa constrictor.

1985, for example, a Dwight Gooden card fresh out of a thirty-five-cent Topps gum pack could be sold for as much as $4 to a dealer. Meanwhile, dealers were getting $5 or more for the card.''

Lemke prefers the occasional oddball card. Few can surpass the recently issued Fleer card showing Atlanta second baseman Glenn Hubbard with a real boa constrictor wrapped over his shoulder. ''The card sells for five cents now,'' Lemke told me late in 1985, ''but will bring $2 to $3 in the future.''

Cards that see limited distribution or are suddenly withdrawn from circulation for one

Front and back of the Nettles error card.

reason or another are also good candidates for a quick return on the dollar. In 1981, the Granny Goose potato chip company put out a special edition of fifteen Oakland A's cards, issuing one to a bag. One card, picturing player Dave Revering, became difficult to acquire soon after Granny Goose stopped distributing it: It seems Dave got traded right after the chips first hit the shelves. Collectors sensed a rarity and began buying up all the Granny Goose chips they could find. The company reportedly even received a call from one Los Angeles collector who asked to have a truckload of 800 cases of potato chips dumped on his lawn.

A 1985 Topps series, which saw limited distribution, were a set of thirty-three 5-by-7-inch plastic cards in 3-D. ''The player figures were embossed out of the background,'' Lemke explained. ''All players in the set were superstars or hot rookies, and the cards were very attractive.'' The cards were sold for fifty cents apiece, but Lemke predicts that the limited nature of the cards will see their prices ''climb significantly'' in coming years.

Another good prospect, reported Lemke, are the unopened cases of cards that dealers purchase directly from the manufacturers and subsequently sell to collectors. Calling their purchase by collectors ''blue-chip speculation,'' he advises collectors to purchase these only for ''long-term appreciation,'' much as one would a savings bond. ''A case of cards can be bought for $175 to $200 from a hobby dealer,'' he said. This will give you between 10,000 to 12,000 cards, depending if you purchase ''wax packs'' or vendor boxes. ''I bought five cases of Topps cards in 1985,'' Lemke said, ''and sorted them down into complete sets. The value of complete Topps sets of recent years have increased 20 percent or so a year.'' Lemke also indicated that unopened cases can also hold untold treasures. For example, in 1985 he also bought cases of cards manufactured by the Donruss company. ''They had already been made up into sets,'' he explained. ''It turned out that there were some variation cards that were corrected in that set (a wrong picture on Tom Seaver's cards, for instance), and the value has already risen from the $11.25 a set I paid to between $22 and $24.''

Error cards can always be counted on to generate interest with collectors, and the 1980s have produced a good crop of these printed bloopers. The scarcest of the contemporary error cards was one issued by the Fleer Chewing Gum Company in 1981 as part of its regular series sold in packs of seventeen for thirty cents a pack at candy counters. A card picturing Graig Nettles, third baseman for the New York Yankees, incorrectly identified as ''Craig'' Nettles on the flip side of the card. The error was spotted by Fleer during the first press run of the cards. The printer stopped the presses, corrected the mistake, and continued with the run. As it turned out. one out of every thirty-three Nettles cards distributed contained the improper spelling of his first name. The demand for the card was responsible for the cards turning up at a Philadelphia sports collectors show that year with the price tags as high as $20.

The Nettles card was perhaps the rarest of numerous errors seen in 1981, a great year for error collectors. The chain of events leading to the wide-scale goofs was set in motion in July 1980 when a Federal Court ruled that the king of cards, Topps, had conspired with the Major League Baseball Players Association to create a monopoly in the exclusive right to depict major-league players on its cards in what amounted to a $10-million-a-year industry. The ruling opened the doors for Fleer (which had filed an anti-trust suit) and Donruss to enter the market. In the rush to get their first cards produced and out into kiddies' hands the following year, the first printing of Donruss cards had twenty-six mistakes and the Fleer cards contained twenty-seven errors—most of which were subsequently corrected in later runs. In the Donruss series, the Johnny Ellis card carries the picture of Jamie Walton. Fleer's goofs had Don Hood appearing on Pete Vuckovich's card; infielder Stan Papi mistakenly identified as a pitcher; Tim Flannery's picture "flopped," making him look as if he were batting on the wrong side of the plate—and the list goes on, like a printer's nightmare. With so many error cards printed that year, one still can round up a good assortment of the '81 errors without mortgaging the house. You can expect their prices to increase steadily over the next decade.

Another headliner of 1981 was the forty-nine-day baseball strike. This single event created a host of collector's items. Some 77,000 All-Star game tickets were sold for the annual classic to be held in Cleveland on July 14, 1981, a game that was cancelled during the strike. The game was rescheduled for August 9, once the strike was settled. Many ticket holders simply bought a new ticket, feeling that the collectable value of the original ticket—documenting baseball's longest strike—was worth more than the refund value. Collectors also say that newspaper headlines and magazine stories printed during the strike, documenting the Baseball Players Association's arbitration, will be turning up with premium prices at collectors shows in the years to come. One bright spot to come out of the strike was expressed by a Phoenix, Arizona, operator of a sports memorabilia shop, who said that business boomed in small sports shops around the country during the strike; fans

49-day baseball strike T-shirt.

were bored when the games weren't being played and wandered into shops to pass the time. Among the items many of them purchased when the games resumed were T-shirts announcing "I Survived the 49 Day Baseball Strike."

The Olympics

Olympic games always create an avalanche of souvenirs in the countries where they are held. When the XXIIIrd Olympiad took place in Los Angeles in the summer of 1984, this country witnessed one of the largest unloading of merchandise since the Bicentennial had the American eagle and the Liberty Bell appearing on everything from souvenir coins to boxes of tissue paper. The enthusiasm was heightened by the fact that it was the first summer games in which the United States had participated in eight years. American teams boycotted the Moscow Olympics in 1980 on the heels of then President Carter's protest of Soviet human rights policies in general and the war in Afghanistan in particular. The U.S.S.R. consequently stayed home during the summer '84 games. One souvenir of the '80 Summer Olympics that has been experiencing steady sales in this country in the years since is the hard-to-find pin from the boycotted event, featuring the official mascot of the Moscow games, an innocuously lovable Russian bear named Misha. Olympic collectors attest to the fact that pin collecting represents one of the fastest growing categories of interest in the collecting field. Whenever Olympic games are held, no matter where, hordes of pin collectors show up, exchanging team pins, official souvenir pins, and national pins, communicating with each other by sign language to get around the language barrier. Because of this country's stance on the

Moscow games, American pin collectors found it difficult to secure those commemorating the Summer 1980 Olympics.

That's where Stanley Jaksina of Providence, Rhode Island, comes in. Jaksina, a dealer in Olympic "mascot" pins, acquired a cache of the Misha the bear pins from a friend who was "stuck" with them after the games were boycotted. He had success selling them in this country through ads in national collecting journals. A lot were sold to Olympic collectors, as might be expected, but, surprisingly, "people who collect bear collectibles also bought Misha pins," he explained. Jaksina said that Misha pins were marketed at the Lake Placid Winter Games in 1980, along with the more plentiful

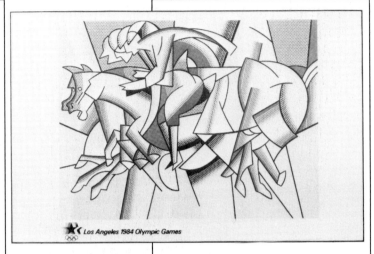

Los Angeles 1984 Olympic Games

Los Angeles games posters.

1988 Olympics memorabilia is already on sale.

Rocky Raccoon items (the raccoon was mascot of the Lake Placid games). It appears that countries strive to outdo each other in the "cute" department when it comes to selecting Olympic mascots. Jaksina pointed out a Goofy Olympics pin, showing the famous Disney dog holding a torch. "In 1980, France chose him to be its Olympic mascot," he said. "These pins are also popular with Disney collectors. A wolf served as the mascot for the Winter Games in Sarajevo in 1984, while the Koreans have already introduced their mascot for the 1988 games—a tiger cub named Hodori (which means 'small tiger' in Korean)."

However, it will be Sam the eagle, designed for the Los Angeles Olympics by the Dis-

Los Angeles Summer Olympics pins, keychains.

Frisbee, cap, and drinking glasses from XIII rd Olympiad.

height of the 1984 Olympic mania. There are fewer of these produced, compared to the mass-market souvenirs, and purist collectors feel that the official documents of the games are closer to the actual event and cut through much of the hoopla.

The 1984 Olympics were certainly not short on hoopla.

ney studios, who will be the best remembered of the Olympic menagerie in this country. During 1984, Sam was everywhere—on stick pins, buttons, key chains, T-shirts, cups, hats, you name it. Sam shared the spotlight with the other official emblem of the games, the "Star In Motion" design. Olympic collectors say, with all due appreciation to Sam, that the items from the L.A. Olympics most likely to stand apart from the mass of memorabilia are things from the actual games—official programs, special passes, tickets, and Olympic postcards mailed home by visitors to the games. These types of items dated from the 1932 Los Angeles Games commanded the highest prices during the

Souvenirs ranged in price from less than a dollar for a Star In Motion pen to several thousands of dollars for a fourteen-karat gold-and-diamond pocket watch. It may take years for all these to whittle down before scarcities emerge. The items most likely to get a head start on this process are those that were produced in limited quantities to start with—commemorative posters and plates, limited-issue coins, framed sets of pins, and beer steins. Knapp Communications issued special limited-edition signed posters for the games, which featured the work of fifteen major contemporary artists. The limited-edition versions of the posters, which sold for $250 each, all contained Olympic themes and were chosen as official posters by the Los Angeles Olympic Organizing Committee. These include works by such artists as Roy Lichtenstein, Robert Rauschenberg, David Hockney, and Jennifer Bartlett, and the photographer Garry Winogrand. Unsigned, unlimited versions of the posters retailed for $30. Mexican-born Rudy Escalera was selected by the organizing committee as the official Commemorative Plate Artist. His series comprised nine plates, including a "Tribute" plate featuring a

1984 Olympics gold coin.

collage of athletes in action and highlighting a woman torchbearer. The remaining plates in the series spotlighted various athletic competitions. The key "Tribute" plate was produced and fired for a limited time period, while the additional eight plates were limited to 19,500 sets worldwide, "making the series truly a valued collector's set," opined *Collectors Mart,* a limited edition art periodical.

The Los Angeles games even made for a bit of numismatic history when the Bureau of the Mint struck the first U. S. gold coin produced in fifty years—since the United States went off the gold standard. The 1984 gold coin honored on its obverse Olympiad XXIII with the image of a male and a female runner jointly carrying a torch aloft. It was anticipated that two million

$10 gold pieces would be produced. The new coin caused a frenzy of excitement in the numismatic community. It was not only the first gold American coin in half a century, but also part of a three-coin series marking the first time Olympic coins were made in the United States. The only way one could obtain the gold coin was to buy it in conjunction with two others, both silver "double-struck" proofs (the standard method for producing high-quality coins). One features a discus thrower, while the Olympic sculpture in front of the Los Angeles coliseum graces the other. The two silver coins could be purchased separately for $32 apiece, or together with the gold coin for $416. Additional Olympic commemoratives were minted, including unlimited quantities of 1983 Olympic silver dollars, bearing a Philadelphia Mint mark, for $28. Three 1983 uncirculated silver coins, originating from the mints in San Francisco, Philadelphia, and Denver, were sold as a "Collector's Set" for $89. Only 600,000 were produced. A "Prestige Set," which encompassed proof coins of all American coinage in the 1983 series—penny, nickel, dime, quarter, and half-dollar, as

well as the Olympic silver dollar—was marketed for $59. The coins proved to be popular, with their sales resulting in a profit of $72 million.

The official sponsors of the Los Angeles games (companies gain this status by donating money, personnel, or products to the Olympics to assist the U. S. teams) all proclaimed their sponsorship on their products or through special promotional pieces. United Airlines was the official airline of the games, with flight crews wearing limited-produced pins during the summer that read: "We are United behind the 1984 U. S. Olympic Team." McDonald's was the official fast-food restaurant and produced a number of short-term promotional items during the games, including "The Ronald McDonald Coloring Calendar of

United Airlines 1984 Olympics pinback.

the 1984 Olympic Games." Commercial items of this kind can also be expected to do well in the future.

The final word on the Los Angeles games might be this: a lot of people made a lot of money during the games. The final tally showed that the 1984 Olympics in Los Angeles made a profit of $225 million. That's a lot of licensee contracts sold, which results in a lot of souvenirs distributed. As these were the first summer Olympic games held in this country in over fifty years, Olympiad XXIII will endure for Americans as one of the memorable sports events of the century. Save something you like and let history do the rest.

9. Kid's Stuff

It's been said that the first things taken away from us in life are our toys. It has also been said that many collectors seem intent on spending the rest of their lives getting the toys back. This is pointed up by the fact that more than half of the hottest collectibles of the twentieth century are items originally targeted toward children: Mickey Mouse clocks, Superman comic books, Shirley Temple dolls, Hopalong Cassidy holster sets. These items have generated some of the greatest attention and highest prices in the collectibles field over the past decade as the kids of the 1930s, '40s, and '50s reached the expendable income brack-

Rubik's Cube jigsaw puzzle.

Rubik's Cube: the Davy Crockett cap of the '80s.

The Simple Solution to Rubik's Cube.

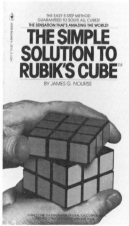

et and began turning up at collector shows and auction galleries, prepared to buy back their toys at whatever price it costs. It stands to reason that the children of the '80s will be no less immune to nostalgia as they begin to approach middle age after the turn of the next century. By that time, Hopalong Cassidy will have been relegated to the history books, replaced by a new generation of high-priced kiddie collectibles. In this distant future, Kermit the Frog will be a king.

"Remember these?" a misty-eyed adult of fifty will

someday ask his wife as they wander through the flea markets of the future. "They called these Rubik's Cubes. A kid in my fourth-grade class—Nathan Urquhart—could get all the colors together in ten minutes. I hated him. Wait, what are these...? Deely bobbers! You put them on your head! We were all wearing them at summer camp back in '82. God, they used to cost a buck and a half back then. Just look at that price: $35! Wow, this one has a Pac-Man on the end of it. Remember Pac-Man and all those arcades? There was this funny-looking kid in the fifth grade—Josiah Clifford; he once got a score of 400,000 on one of those crazy machines. Hey, look, a box of Transformers! Honey, quick, give me my wallet!"

Dolls

Some say nostalgia begins in the crib, which may explain why dolls continue to be one of the most popular forms of collectibles and consistently command the highest prices across the board. With the success of character dolls to date (Shirley Temple dolls from the '30s sell for as much as $750), one might consider the merits of the Brooke Shields doll, which hit the market in 1982. Made by LJN

Brooke Shields doll depicting "The World's Most Glamorous Teenager."

of New York, the doll came dressed in a pink and gray cowl-neck sweater suit and white boots, and was billed on the box as "The World's Most Glamorous Teenager." The promotion copy went on to describe Brooke as "a multi-talented, beautiful young lady who's captured the hearts and dreams of the young world," adding, "she's now a dazzling glamorous 11 1/2-inch tall fully poseable real living fashion doll." Each living doll came with a star-shaped plastic ring, hairbrush, posing stand, and "personally autographed" picture of the winsome Miss Shields. It's fair to say that not since Twiggy has a teenage fashion model attracted as much attention as Brooke Shields; her place in the '80s seems secure. Selling for about $8 when new, the teenage Brooke Shields doll was already capable of pulling twice that by the time Miss Shields celebrated her twenty-first birthday in 1986.

Perhaps the most unusual doll to hit the market, and one that will certainly be remembered for the storm of controversy it generated, was the Rambo doll, which hit toy store shelves just before the Christmas season in 1985. The doll, produced by Coleco Industries Inc. of Connecticut, was inspired by the box office exploits of Sylvester Stallone's Rambo character. The second Rambo film, *Rambo: First Blood Part II,* was the hottest movie of the summer '85 season, netting a whopping $140 million at the box office during its first three months of release. "We believe that the Rambo character is emerging as a new American hero," Bar-bara Wruck, a Coleco vice president, was quoted as saying in the *Boston Globe* when the new toy was announced. "He is a hero and a justice-seeking individual, and those are characteristics that we all want, including the children who will play with the dolls." This would be the perfect doll of the Reagan era, Coleco indicated, with Wruck citing President Reagan's comment after the release of American hostages held by Shiite Moslems: "Boy, after seeing *Rambo* last night, I know what to do the next time this happens." Some were predicting that Rambo would outdo G.I. Joe in the male macho doll market. Hasbro Inc., makers of G.I. Joe, didn't see it that way. A company spokesman was quoted as remarking, "Rambo has only one character. G.I. Joe has a range of personalities, specialties, and functions." Competition from G.I. Joe turned out to be the least of Rambo's problems. A few weeks before Christmas, a group of parents marched in front of Coleco's West Hartford headquarters, carrying signs protesting the release of the new Rambo dolls. "The character of Rambo makes war and killing exciting to kids," one protester told UPI. Some of the protest signs read

"Killer in the Toybox." In the end, however, the negative publicity didn't seem to hurt sales. Hundreds of thousands of Rambo dolls, priced at under $10, joined Rambo comic books, bubble gum cards, and coloring books as some of the most popular items in Junior's stocking that Christmas.

It was Coleco that made doll history in 1983 when it marketed the Cabbage Patch doll. Its debut was very different from Rambo's: at that time, parents were coming to fisticuffs to get one of the dolls. The Cabbage Patch doll soon earned the title of the most popular toy of the age. "What a Doll!" *Newsweek* proclaimed in a cover story on the Cabbage Patch craze in its December 12, 1983, issue. For anyone who has just returned from a journey to the Horsehead Nebula, here is the story of the cuddly kids in a nut shell: once upon a time there was a Georgia sculptor named Xavier Roberts who went out to the cabbage patch one day and found a gold mine. His original handmade dolls, inspired by the work of local folk artists, employed a cloth head resembling a cabbage with eyes and a couple of well-placed stitches for dimples. They featured a gimmick as old as mankind itself: no two were exactly alike. Each doll was different from the next, made so by variations of color in hair, eyes, and skin, addition of freckles, style of clothes, placement of dimples—just like real kids. And they also had names, identified with the "adoption papers" that came with each doll. Roberts fitted his Cleveland, Georgia, shop with the decor of a maternity ward, called Babyland General Hospital, complete with sales clerks dressed as doctors and nurses and dolls displayed in incubators and bassinets. For Roberts, who affixed a signature to each sale, the cash registers were ringing to the tune of anywhere from $125 to $1000 per doll when Coleco came knocking at his door.

Coleco was flushed from success in the video game field and the dolls were a marked departure for the company. They were also viewed by the industry as something of a gamble. Would the public take to a doll with a face that only a mother could love? Would the adoption papers guarantee that each owner felt the responsibility of a mother or father when given the doll as a gift? In preliminary testing during the fall of 1982, Coleco became sure that it had the greatest attraction since the lollipop. But even they could not have anticipated the degree of success soon to be accorded the dolls. After months of anticipation and pre-release media hype, the public was ready, cash in hand, when the first Coleco Cabbage Patch Kids, bearing $25 price tags, hit stores in November. Almost immediately, Coleco announced that it had sorely underestimated the demand and as a result was doubtful that there would be enough of the kids to go around before Christmas, despite the fact that the company's plants in Hong Kong were cranking them out like cole slaw at a rate of 200,000 per week. All this fueled pub-

Cabbage Patch Kids cereal box.

First issue of the Cabbage Patch Kids *magazine.*

lic hysteria to the point that many stores were the scene of near riots during the holiday shopping season as adults grappled for the precious few dolls. To avoid mob scenes, some stores opted to sell their allotments one doll at a time to people who waited in line as long as fourteen hours for the pleasure of taking home a Cabbage Patch Kid. Cabbage Patch scalpers hung around in front of leading toy stores and mall parking lots, offering to resell dolls for as much as $150. Before long, Cabbage Patch counterfeits emerged. Two men were arrested in New York after they had sold some 500 of the fake dolls to a private investigator. Police say that the pair had dispensed of over 30,000 of the dolls before their arrest. The dolls continued to be hot right through 1984 and '85, with retail sales for Cabbage Patch Kids products totaling $540 million for just the first five months of 1985—the same year that *Cabbage Patch Kids Magazine* first hit the newsstand.

So what about the future of these dolls: are they investibles or just cuddly vegetables? There was no question at the mid-decade point that Cabbage Patch dolls were making an impact on the collecting field. Ads for Cabbage Patch dolls accounted for more than a third of all doll-related classifieds appearing in the *Antique Trader Weekly.* Obviously, most popular are the original creations of Xavier Roberts. The earliest, a 1978 Roberts doll of a boy and girl (the girl's in a christening gown) are priced at $1650 each, while a 1981 boy doll, signed by the creator, rings in at $450. Coleco's Kids are also getting premium prices, with one Maryland advertiser running down the following list and accompanying prices: 1983 Coleco's $75 to $165; with glasses, $85; bald, with tooth, $85; twins with pacifiers, $150; with tooth and

The Bialosky bear.

dressed in lion or deer outfit, $95. Another ad had a Coleco Cabbage Patch freckled girl from '83 priced at $175, while a 1985 boy, described as "bald, big ears," was tagged at $65. It remains to be seen if such prices will outlast the fad, but serious doll collectors expect to be contending with Cabbage Patch mania for many years to come.

Teddy Bears

Some dolls never go out of fashion. One of the most popular of the '80s also ranks as one of the most enduring: the Teddy Bear. During the 1980s the Teddy Bear market exploded, due to many factors—not the least of which was an aggressive promotional campaign by Workman Publishing of New York after the release of the *Teddy Bear Catalog* by Peggy and Alan Bialosky in 1980.

History records that the first Teddy Bear originated via a political cartoon in the November 16, 1906, edition of the *Washington Post,* which made light of President Teddy Roosevelt's refusal to shoot a captured bear during a hunting trip, saying that to do so would be most unsportsmanlike. The incident prompted a Brooklyn couple, Morris and Rose Michtom, to produce a new cute bear for children. They received permission from none other than TR himself to call their stuffed animals Teddy Bears. It was the birth of the Ideal toy company, America's leading producer of Teddy Bears. The European Teddy Bear was being created about the same time by the Steiff Company of Germany.

Ideal no longer produces Teddy Bears, while Steiff continues to produce what has been called the Rolls Royce of Teddies all these many years. (150,000 Steiff bears were purchased in this country in 1982, a rise of over 50 percent from the preceding year.) Steiff owes much of its brisk sales to the Bialoskys and Workman Publishing, who brought Ted-

dy Bear buyers (70 percent identified as adults buying for adults) out of the closet to the point that Teddies became one of the chic toys of the 1980s. The Bialoskys, pet columnists for the *Cleveland Plain Dealer,* had been collecting bears for a dozen years when they were approached by Workman with the idea of authoring a catalog documenting the Teddy Bear phenomenon over the years. The book turned out to be a runaway bestseller for the New York publisher and generated all sorts of new Teddy products, from the annual Teddy Bear Calendar to notepads and assorted stationery products, Christmas orna-

The Teddy Bear Catalog *by Peggy and Alan Bialosky.*

ments, Jigsaw puzzles, and prerequisite T-shirts. After the first Teddy Bear Calendar sold out in 1982, Workman began an annual contest in which it asked people to submit snapshots of their teddies for consideration in the following year's calendar art. More than 10,000 entries were received for the 1984 calendar contest, with the winning bears flown to New York for a photo session. The Teddy craze reached new heights when 25,000 people converged on the Philadelphia Zoo in June 1983 for the second American Bear Rally. All sorts of bears, old and new, were on hand. A miniature Teddy Bear named Waldo was shot out of a cannon, while 1000 people entered their bears in assorted contests. The winner of the "most loved bear" was one reduced to a paw and some stuffing, allegedly after a lifetime of cuddling.

Joining the Steiff bears are new lines of Teddies produced to cater to the increasing demand. As could be expected, the Bialoskys have emerged with their own bear, called, appropriately enough, the Bialosky Bear. It features a long muzzle and arms, with oversized feet, and is said to have been modeled after a 1907 German model. Produced by Gund Inc., the Bialosky bears sell for $10 to $50. Meanwhile, new Steiffs range from $12.98 for a 4-inch bear with swivel head to $600 for a 3-foot mohair Steiff. A Concord, Massachusetts, specialty shop, Bear-In-Mind, marketed for $500 an 18-inch reproduction of the original 1903 Steiff Teddy Bear, called Papa Steiff, which was produced in the early '80s by Steiff in a limited edition of 7000. Bear-In-Mind called it "a sound investment." House of Collectibles' *Official 1986 Price Guide to Antiques and Other Collectibles* observed that "the modern Teddy Bears are fast disappearing off the store shelves and look to be the collectibles of the future." Bearmania went a little too far when it was reported that basketball player Kareem Abdul-Jabbar filed suit in 1985 against a Chicago firm who was marketing a Teddy Bear garbed in basketball gear and named "Kareem Abdul-Jabear."

The Video Game Phenomenon

While many of their parents were off to Teddy Bear rallies during the early '80s, kids could be found down at the neighborhood arcade feeding quarters into video game ma-

chines. I remember in 1983 spotting what might have been the first classified ad for souvenirs from the video game era. "Wanted: Tokens from video game arcades," it read. It's inevitable that people would seek keepsakes from the great video game fad of the early '80s. It was a full-scale phenomenon that began back in the Cro-Magnon Period of Pong and advanced millennia during the early '80s thanks to Space Invaders, Asteroids, Pac-Man, and Ms. Pac-Man, only to go into a tailspin by the time Baby Pac-Man hit arcades in 1983. While it lasted, its impact on this country was remarkable.

Burned into my memory was the scene I took in one day in the spring of 1981. I was

Pac-Man T-shirt, notebook, and drinking mug.

in Ocean City, New Jersey, attending a baseball card convention and decided to get some fresh air by going for a stroll along the boardwalk. It was then that I heard a sound not unlike that of a locust invasion: the combined zapping and munching of thousands of arcade machines being played in unison. Open-fronted arcades lined the boardwalk as far as the eye could see in either direction. This was the great summer of Pac-Man. I went in one arcade and ventured a quarter on the game. I lasted thirty seconds before I was swallowed by a creature named Blinky. A kid standing nearby, who was up to 112,000 points and hardly sweating, explained to me as he played that it was all a matter of figuring out the "pattern" and memorizing it. Over the next year, I became hooked. A couple of compatriots and I dumped hundreds of

dollars into Pac-Man games wherever we could find them, which was everywhere—bars, airports, restaurants, laundries, bowling alleys, convenience stores. Before I retired from the game, I could take on any ten-year-old in town. Even now I cringe as I think of how many quarters I sacrificed to Blinky, Pinky, and Clyde.

The fact is that in 1981 Americans dropped $5 billion worth of quarters into arcade video game slots, with most going into Pac-Man machines. Other popular games included Defender, Donkey Kong, Robotron, Centipede, Dig-Dug, and Q-Bert. But it was Midway's Pac-Man that offered the greatest assortment of spinoff products. An outfit called Uniprints reportedly paid Midway

Pac-Man portfolio.

an advance of $100,000 for the rights to produce Pac-Man T-shirts. Following in quick pursuit of success soon came Pac-Man drinking mugs, $5 visor caps, Pac-Man air fresheners, ties (made by a company

Party plates sporting Pac-Man.

How To Win At Pac-Man *guide.*

Video Swapper *magazine featuring Pac-Man.*

called Video Babies), bumper stickers ("I Brake For Pac-Man"), and a handheld home version made by Coleco. A book, *How To Win At Pac-Man,* written by the editors of *Consumer Guide,* was a best-seller in 1982. One of its tips: "Get to know the monsters, their personalities and reactions." In January 1982, a song called "Pac-Man Fever," recorded on Columbia by Buckner and Garcia, climbed the charts. Meanwhile, *Video Games,* just one of the many new video game magazines to be rushed onto the market in 1982, mimicked a *Time* magazine cover on its premiere issue by honoring Pac-Man as "Man of the Year." Even the traditional game industry jumped on the bandwagon; in 1982 Milton Bradley shamelessly introduced the Pac-Man board game. It neither blinked nor gulped.

An entire industry flourished in home games, with Atari, Activision, and Intellivision shooting for the home market with games based not only on the popular arcade versions, but also hundreds of others sporting names like Stampede, Laser Blast, Dodge 'Em, and Kaboom! In March 1982, Activision, which saw its sales grow from $6 million to over $60 million in three years, shipped out over one million home video game cartridges during the month of March 1982 alone. What this all means is a lot of cartridges circulated during the early '80s. Which of these are likely to generate the greatest interest to future collectors?

A safe play would be to go with games based on familiar pop culture heroes, such as the special-edition Superman game program released by Atari. Others which will find future interest are those that cashed in on major motion pictures of the era. The first of these film-to-game conversions was the *Empire Strikes Back* cartridge, produced by Parker Brothers and playable

Ms. Pac-Man wind-up toy.

137

on Atari systems. The ultimate of this genre, however, came when Intellivision made a game-film-game leap of sorts by releasing a cartridge inspired by *Tron,* the Disney movie about a man who gets trapped in a video game.

During the height of the video game craze, a number of clubs for gamers flourished, under the direction of the individual manufacturers. Each had its own quarterly newsletter. "Atari Age," the official newsletter of the Atari Game Club, debuted in the spring of 1981 with a story about a Southern Californian who won a Space Invaders tourney with a score of 165,200. Activision's newsletter came forth in the fall of 1981, while "Odyssey Adventure" premiered in the winter 1982. "Intellivision News" began the same year. Official newsletters such as these, which document a phenomenon from within, traditionally do well in collecting circles, and one might expect complete runs of these periodicals to emerge as some of the most desirable reminders of the video game explosion. The future bodes well for video games as collectibles, according to Dana Hawkes, head of the Collectibles Department at Sotheby's in New York. "Because of its brief history, they

The Dazzler *fought crime on roller skates.*

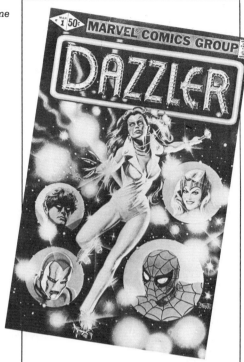

will be as popular as 1940s jukeboxes are today," Hawkes told me.

One of the legacies of video games may be the familiarity with computers that it provided to kids barely out of diapers. This connection was carried further in 1983 when a British publishing company began publishing the world's first computer comic. ECC Publication's "Load Runner" reportedly dealt with loading software programs, as well as a wealth of computer facts and features mixed in with comic storylines.

She-Hulk *comic book.*

The Comics

In this country, however, comic books were going through their own transitional period. One of the major developments was the emergence of women superheroes in the funny books, in a direct appeal to interest girls in the superhero comic book field, which, with the exception of Wonder Woman and Supergirl, had largely been considered male terrain. Marvel Comics enlisted some of its biggest guns in the effort, including Stan Lee, who created and wrote the first of "She-Hulk," which appeared in February 1980. In the first episode, lawyer Jennifer Walters receives a blood transfusion from her cousin, one Dr. Banner—known during his off days as the Hulk. The blood transfusion saves Jennifer's life, but it has one side effect ... The exploits of another Marvel superwoman of the '80s are documented in issues of "Dazzler." Dazzler, who debuted in March 1981, fights crime on disco roller skates. The "Dazzler" comics were viewed as a big hit in the industry, with Marvel Editor-In-Chief Jim Shooter saying that the success of their skating superwoman heralded an end to the long-held belief that, when it came to superheroes, "women don't sell."

Yesterday's fashion queen came back in this Katy Keene Special.

Copies of the first few issues in the series had already quadrupled in value over the original cover price by mid-decade.

A woman of an entirely different sort experienced a revival during the '80s when Katy Keene, comic fashion queen of the '50s, was revived. Until Katy was discontinued by Archie Comics in 1961, she served as a role model for thousands of youngsters, who followed her exploits in a series penned by cartoonist Bill Woggon. Katy was the perfect "reader participation" publication, with readers sending in fashion ideas for Katy and her friends.

Largely through the efforts of a group of Katy's original readers (now pushing middle age), who had banded together to form a fan club joined by a quarterly newsletter called "Katy Keene Magazine," the comic's favorite clotheshorse reemerged during the '80s. Woggon, now in his seventies and living in California, designed a Katy Keene cover for Overstreet's 1984–85 *Comic Book Price Guide.* Also, Archie/Red Circle Comics issued a thirty-three-page Katy Keene Special No. 1 in September 1983. The issue featured reprinted stories, paper dolls, and pinups dating from 1950–1961. It was the talk of the annual Katy-Kon convention held in San Diego that year, with members buying out copies as they appeared. The current generation of comic buyers, however, could not relate to the '50s fashions they found in the first issue, and Archie quickly modernized Katy. Out went the letter sweaters and leopard loungers, to be replaced by Calvin Kleins and aerobics outfits. Regardless of how well Katy adapts to the '80s, her legion of original fans will assure that her contemporary incarnations will join the ranks of early editions on many want lists for decades to come.

3-D comic book with glasses.

Another flashback to the '50s came in the form of 3-D. Early in the '80s 3-D was being re-heralded like the Second Coming, but a couple of bad movies (including a simply awful spaghetti western called *Comin' At Ya!*) and the major box office disappointment of *Jaws 3-D* when it was released during the summer of 1983 all but killed whatever hope there was for a revival. During the boomlet, however, comic book companies brought out some new 3-D comics, including a line published by 3D Cosmic Publications of North Hollywood. The first such comic debuted in 1982 and came with the mandatory cardboard glasses. Featuring the art of Jack Kirby, it was titled "Battle For a Three Dimensional World." As far as the '80s were concerned, it was a losing battle. But with 3-D comics from the '50s now fetching from $60 to $200 in top condition, it certainly wouldn't hurt to stash away a couple of their '80s counterparts.

Comic collecting is largely an esoteric affair, ranking with science fiction and baseball cards as the field encompassing the most intense collectors to be found in the collecting world today. Most comic book collectors readily admit that they are all but consumed by their hobby. To enter a comic book convention is to venture into a limboland almost untouched by the outside world. Comic book buffs communicate through periodicals tailored for their interest. A leader in the field is *Comic Collector,* co-edited by Don and Maggie Thompson and published by Krause Publications of Iola, Wisconsin. In September 1985, the *New York Post* asked the Thompsons which of the comics of the '80s will have the greatest future market potential. Among their predictions were "Spiderman" No. 252 (in which the old web-spinner received a new

costume), Marvel's "G.I. Joe" No. 1 (dated June 1982, printed on Baxter paper and available only by direct sale), the comic book version of *Revenge of the Jedi* (later changed to *Return of the Jedi*), and the first run of the initial issue of "Teenage Mutant Ninga Turtles."

Plastic Creatures

Halfway through the '80s, it appeared that toy stores around the country were being taken over by aliens from another world. What started with *Star Wars* was nothing short of an invasion by mid-decade, when the ruler of toy stores was Megatron. Selling for $22.97, Megatron is a member of Hasbro Inc.'s Transformer line. It took Megatron and his fellow Hasbro Transformers to finally dethrone the Cabbage Patch Kids at the top of the list of bestselling toys, as published by *Toy & Hobby World.* Transformers, in case you're lacking a seven-year-old in the family, are toys that start out looking like one thing, often a vehicle of some sort, and with a couple of twists and turns of jointed parts, reminiscent of the wrist action employed on a Rubik's Cube, they are transformed into something else completely—towering multi-armed monsters are quite popular here. The Japanese actually invented Transformer-type toys in 1983; they were displayed at the Tokyo Toy Fair that spring and called Machine Men. The manufacturer, Bandai, was unsuccessful in getting the toys introduced into this country. That step was taken by the Tonka Corporation of Minnesota, which purchased rights to produce a similar line in the United States under the name Go-Bots. It pulled all stops in getting the new line introduced to America's kiddies back in January 1984, including making GoBots a basis of a comic book series, an extensive television campaign aired on Saturday mornings, and a promotional tie-in with Cookie Crisps cereal. That spring, however, Hasbro entered the field with its Transformers. Throughout the summer, the battle of the changeable robots raged at toy counters around the nation. By the end of 1984, the GoBots and Transformers had each racked up sales surpassing $100 million. Transformers and GoBots both received substantial back-up support from weekly animated series on television. The third entry in the robot sweepstakes, the Voltron series, came about when Match-

box Toys took an existing weekly cartoon program and designed a line of toys around it.

Transformers began edging out its competition early in 1985. With success came one of the hottest license spinoff logos of the Christmas '85 season. Youngsters that year could be outfitted in Transformers slippers, thermal underwear, warm-up coordinates, boots, swimsuits, and watches, to name just a few. All totaled, fifty-one different companies were producing 121 products bearing the Transformers logo. That spells success, in any language.

Robots have a long history of popularity with collectors, who rank them among the most desirable toys of the '50s. Kids of the '80s will certainly reserve a special place in their hearts for the robots of today. Those likely to be the more difficult to acquire will be the higher-priced models. Department stores sold enough Voltron III Robots for $12.99 to fill a small galaxy during the Christmas 1985 season. Far fewer of the deluxe Voltron III models were sold, largely due to their high price—$59.99. The deluxe set is actually made up of five robots that when combined in something out of a space-age cheerleader routine, form the ultimate Voltron. Going for only the best was the suggestion expressed by Julie Collier, head of the Collectibles Department of Christie's East in New York. "Since millions of these have been made and they're the top-selling toy in America right now," Collier told me in the fall of 1985, "I would suggest buying only the best examples to save. They're so imaginative and clever, I have a feeling future generations of collectors will find them fascinating too."

Where this will all lead is uncertain, but one thing is sure: the toy industry isn't through with robots yet.

10. What's Ahead?

The collecting future is here now.

All the Presidents up to the year 2021 are alive at this very moment, though a few may only be cutting their baby teeth in hometowns that will someday be inundated with tourists looking for souvenirs.

The hottest baseball card of the year 2006 is in our midst right now, and you can still have it for pocket change. It will be selling for hundreds of dollars twenty years from now. It is the rookie card for some ballplayer who will set the sports world on its ears by toppling a long-standing professional baseball record.

In opposite corners of the country right now, two people are about to be told in so many words "you ought to be in pictures." Those words will prompt both to give up their jobs at the Schmucker's coffee shop and Joe's filling station before the end of the year. Both will go on to win Academy Awards by 1999.

Meanwhile, a struggling writer is completing a script for a commercial pitching dog food. This person will someday write the script for a film to rival *Gone With the Wind*.

You don't have to be a psychic to know that the future is nothing more than the present being played out. What makes the game of collecting so intriguing is trying to second-guess the future—with the rewards going to the collector with the gumption to stockpile tomorrow's collectibles before anyone else does. Granted, it's all easier said than done. You can start today by buying up every baseball card being printed, in hopes that you have a future winner on your hands. Reality is that as America approaches the last dozen years of the twentieth century, it is difficult to anticipate what personalities and events will influence our lives in the next century. Difficult, but not entirely impossible.

For example, as we have seen, anniversaries have a knack of unleashing a host of souvenirs. The late '80s and 1990s will see the anniversaries of several events that have changed our lives. Each will be accompanied by a supply of souvenirs ranging from the ridiculous to the sublime. Other events can be anticipated to a considerable degree, although the exact dates of these cannot be affixed: the coronation of the next monarch of Great Britain, for example. Barring death or abdication, that person will be Prince Charles. Consequently, someday all that Royal Wedding stuff will be joined by coronation and jubilee memorabilia. And the beat goes on.

Here are some dates to remember, with apologies to the *World Almanac:*

May 1987. The golden anniversary of the completion of the Golden Gate Bridge. The President will probably be there, and so will a lot of hawkers with souvenirs to sell, with the highest-priced items made of solid gold. Practically everything else will be gilded in plastic.

February 1989. The silver anniversary of the start of Beatlemania. A small group of graying Americans will call for the surviving Beatles to perform in concert together, while most eighth graders will think that Ringo Starr was the name of an outlaw who rode with Jesse James.

April 20, 1989. Two-hundredth anniversary of the inauguration of George Washington as the first President of the United States. The anniversary will prompt the nation's media to scrutinize the institution of the Presidency, and there will probably be a week-long television docudrama called "White House," which will detail the lives and loves of all of our forty-one Chief Executives, with a few historical events thrown in for good measure.

September 1989. The fiftieth anniversary of the beginning of World War II in Europe. This country will take dutiful notice of the date, which will be widely marked in Europe. But for the most part, we will wait until December 7, 1991—the golden anniversary of Pearl Harbor—to observe the occasion. Throughout the early '90s, there will be a widespread nostalgia boom on the '40s as key events of World War II are marked, culminating in 1995 with the half-century anniversaries of the death of Franklin Roosevelt and of the advent of nuclear weaponry.

December 1991. One-hundredth anniversary of the invention of basketball, an occasion which the NBA will make the most of. Most Americans will continue watching football, however.

Summer 1992. If all goes as scheduled, Chicago will host a world's fair this year. Everyone will still be excited about fairs after a rush of fifty-year retrospectives on the New York World's Fair of 1939–40 a couple of years before.

September 1992. The centennial of the invention of the first gasoline automobile. Gasoline-powered vehicles were supposed to have been replaced with electrical cars by now—but don't hold your breath waiting for it to happen.

October 1992. This is the big one: the five hundredth anniversary of Columbus' trip to America. Everyone at this point will roundly agree that Columbus did not discover the New World, but just about everybody (except American Indians) will celebrate nevertheless.

Fall 1997. Television will be marking its fiftieth anniversary. Oldtime viewers will get dewey-eyed as they reminisce about shows like "Miami Vice." Someone will be heard to say, "They just don't make 'em like that anymore."

February 15, 1998. Expect a rush of media self-analysis on the United States' role in the world on the centennial of the sinking of the battleship *Maine*, which sparked the Spanish-American War and ultimately ended America's brief flirt with colonialism. The last Spanish-American War veteran will have died in a nursing home just a few years earlier.

December 1999. The bicentennial of the death of George Washington. A lot of revolutionary retrospectives will be in evidence. Donnie Osmond will be lured out of retirement to play the Founding Father on Broadway.

Unquestionably, the major anticipated event of the next few years will be the arrival of the bimillennium, the year 2000 A.D., an event of colossal proportions as it will be observed the world over. It's a fair guess that bimillennium collectibles will rival anything witnessed in the souvenir field this century. In fact, the first of these souvenirs is already available and has been for a few years now. "It is the only series of commemoratives that has ever been initiated twenty years prior to the event that is being commemorated," Thomas Mulvihill told me, referring to his bronze, silver, and gold bimillennium commemorative medals. Mulvihill, of Cresskill, New Jersey, calls his business MM 2000, named after the Roman and Arabic numerals representing the year 2000. Every December 1 since 1980, Mulvihill's company has issued a coin-size medal commemorating one of twenty individuals culled from twenty centuries who, in Mulvihill's words,

Bimillennium medals featuring Jesus and Galileo.

"have had a positive and significant influence on mankind." The first coin featured the face of Jesus Christ. "Christ was chosen not specifically for the religious significance," the far-sighted entrepreneur explained, "but for the extent to which his existence has had an effect on mankind. Even the very date we write is directly related to his life." Others in the series include Da Vinci, Copernicus, Galileo, Newton, Watt, Pasteur, Bell, Edison, Einstein, and Freud. Mulvihill is banking on the fact that he has a real head start over everyone, keeping his medallions from being lost in the flood of those which will follow. "There will only be a limited number of collectors who had the foresight to begin the series twenty years in advance," he said. "They will have a complete set of medals, while others are scrambling to collect all the memorabilia of the day." Mulvihill is enthusiastic about the importance of the arrival of the year 2000, which he ventures to call "perhaps the greatest single commemorative event in many, many generations," adding that "only one other time since the birth of Christ has Man welcomed a new Millennia."

Mulvihill sent me one of the

first coins issued in 1980, and I must admit that an eerie feeling came over me when I held in my hands an item produced to commemorate an event nearly twenty years in the future. Its existence reflects the ultimate in collecting certainty: an artifact that says, to all and sundry, that our packrat instincts will be alive and well as we enter the twenty-first century.

That thought crossed my mind as I placed my first souvenir of the bimillennium in the same burgeoning box that contains, among other things, a Michael Jackson doll.

Index

Permissions

The author would like to thank these individuals and companies for allowing use of the following copyrighted materials in this book: p. 10, Copyright © 1983, Time Inc. All rights reserved. Reprinted by permission from *Time*; p. 12, *The Life of Pope John Paul*, Copyright Marvel Comics Group. Marvel Comic Book titles and characters are trademarks of the Marvel Comics Group, a division of Cadence Industries Corporation. Super-Heroes is a jointly owned trademark of the Marvel Comics Group; p. 14, Copyright © 1985, National Geographic Society. Used by permission; p. 16, (bottom-right), Reprinted from *Not Quite TV Guide* by Gerald Sussman. Copyright © 1983 by Gerald Sussman. Used by permission of Crown Publishers, Inc.; p. 20, (bottom), Reproduced by kind permission of Royal Mail Stamps and Philately; p. 23, *The Royal Baby: The Private Life of His Royal Highness Prince William*. Text copyright © 1983 by Rollene W. Saal Associates, illustrations copyright © 1983 by Emanuel Schongut. Designed by Sara Giovanitti. Reprinted by permission of Pocket Books, a division of Simon & Schuster, Inc.; p. 27, Permission granted by Richard J. Wagner; p. 30, *Mr. Halley's Comet: Everyone's Complete Guide to Seeing the Celestial Event*, copyright © 1984 Sky Publishing Corp. All rights reserved. Used by permission; pp. 37, 38, Courtesy PSEnterprises; p. 47, Courtesy Martha D. Studhalter; p. 48, Permission granted by Carole Lee, *New York Post*; p. 49, Dover Publications, Inc.; p. 52, Courtesy Liberty Bronze, Inc.; pp. 57–59, Copyrighted by McCormick Distilling Co.; p. 61, World Doll, Brooklyn, NY; 64, Manufactured under license by LJN Toys, Ltd., New York City; p. 77, *Raiders of the Lost Ark:* TM and copyright 1981 Lucasfilm Ltd; pp. 79–80, Copyright Lucasfilm Ltd. (LFL) 1980. All rights reserved. Courtesy of Lucasfilm Ltd., pp. 81–82, Courtesy Ernst Enterprises; p. 85, Starlog Press; p. 87, *The Legend of the Lone Ranger*, Copyright 1981 by Lone Ranger Television, Inc.; p. 90, Copyright by Universal Pictures, a Division of Universal City Studios, Inc. All rights reserved. Courtesy of MCA Publishing Rights, a Division of MCA Inc.; p. 90 (trading cards), Pacific Trading Cards, Inc., Edmonds, WA; p. 91, Copyrighted by Lorimar Productions; 92, Courtesy Royal Orleans; p. 93, Newman's Own, Inc.; p. 98, *Nancy Reagan Fashion Paper Dolls In Full Color*, Dover Publications, Inc.; p. 99, The Last Wound-Up, Inc.; p. 104; Permission granted by A. Wesley Soderstrom; p. 105, Politicards, a product of the Kamber Group; p. 106 (top), Permission granted by Jim D. Warlick, Political Americana; pp. 108–9, Permission Steve Silverman; p. 110 (top), Copyright © 1983 Time Inc. All rights reserved. Reprinted by permission from *Time*, (middle), Copyright © 1983 Newsweek, Inc., (bottom), Reprinted with permission from *TV Guide* Magazine. Copyright © 1983 by Triangle Publications, Inc. Radnor, Pennsylvania; p. 113, Top, Permission granted by Lois Galgay Reckitt, Vice President-Executive, National Organization for Women; p. 116, Hackett American; pp. 117–18, Courtesy Robert Lemke, Baseball Cards magazine; p. 123, Copyright L. A. Olympic Committee; p. 123, (flying disc). This is the exclusive flying disc for the 1984 Olympics. The Trademark Frisbee® is the brand name and trademark of Wham-O, Inc.; p. 127, *The Simple Solution to Rubik's Cube*, Copyright Bantam Books; p. 128, Manufactured under license by LJN Toys, Ltd., New York City; p. 131, The Cabbage Patch Kids are a copyrighted product of Coleco Industries Inc.; p. 133, Copyright © 1980, 1984 Peggy and Alan Bialosky. Workman Publishing, New York; pp. 135–37, Pac-Man is a trademark of Midway Mfg. Co., a Bally Company; p. 136, *How To Win At Pac-Man*, Permission granted by Publications International, LTD. Published by Pocket Books, January 1982. p. 138, *Dazzler* and *The Savage She-Hulk*, Copyright Marvel Comics Group. Marvel Comic Book titles and characters are trademarks of the Marvel Comics Group, a division of Cadence Industries Corporation Industries Corporation. Super-Heroes is a jointly owned trademark of the Marvel Comics Group; p. 139, *Katy Keene Special*, Copyright © 1986 Archie Comic Publications, Inc.; 147, Courtesy Thomas Mulvihill, MM 2000.